This Is Not a Game

This Is Not a Game

DAVE HAYES

dhayesMEDIA

© 2023 Dave Hayes

All rights reserved. This book is protected by the copyright laws of the United States of America. No portion of this book may be stored electronically, transmitted, copied, reproduced or reprinted for commercial gain or profit without prior written permission from **DHayes Media LLC**. Permission requests may be emailed to: **dave@dhayesmedia.com** or through our website contact form at **DHayesMedia.com**

Unless otherwise noted, all scripture quotations taken from the (NASB®) New American Standard Bible®, copyright © 2020 by The Lockman Foundation. Used by permission. All rights reserved. lockman.org.

This book and other **DHayes Media** titles can be found at: **DHayesMedia.com** and **PrayingMedic.com**

For more information email us at: **dave@dhayesmedia.com**

ISBN-13: 978-1-7345525-9-1 (DHayes Media)
Printed in the U.S.A.

DEDICATION

To members of the U.S. armed forces:
The world owes you a debt of gratitude for your
patriotism, dedication and determination
to preserve our freedom.

ACKNOWLEDGMENTS

To the anons and patriots who held the line
and refused to quit when all seemed lost.

TABLE OF CONTENTS

	Introduction 11
	Introduction . . . 11
1	Ten Days Darkness 17
2	Myths and Misconceptions About Q 25
3	Iron Eagle 33
4	Sparrow Red 57
5	We Don't Say His Name 63
6	This Is Not a Game 77
7	The Anatomy of a Smear Campaign 83
8	Taking the Red Pill 95
9	Where We Go One, We Go All 99
10	The Hunt for Red October 105
11	Question and Answer 119
12	Follow the Pen 133
13	Follow the Watch 149
14	Bait Expends Ammunition 155
15	John Durham 167
16	Trust the Plan 177
17	Nothing Can Stop What Is Coming 185
	Glossary 191

NOTE

This book was created without the
use of artificial intelligence.

INTRODUCTION

This book is the third volume in the Q Chronicles—a series covering the messages posted online by the anonymous entity known as Q. It isn't necessary to have read the first two volumes to understand the material presented here; this book stands on its own. But for the benefit of those who are not familiar with Q and those who have not read the first book in this series titled Calm Before the Storm, or the second book titled The Great Awakening, a brief overview of information from those books will be helpful.

Q is an anonymous entity that first posted on the internet message board 4chan in October of 2017. Other internet message boards have been used since the first post. Q provides information to the public. The information comes in various formats, including straightforward written messages, riddles, coded text, links to government documents, news articles, memes, and videos. Hints are provided and questions are asked that help researchers connect various people and organizations to specific events. Millions of people from all walks of life research these topics and report what they've found. When the information is assembled, it reveals the truth about corruption in federal government, the entertainment industry, centers of higher education, the intelligence community, broadcast and social media, and large corporations.

Q claims to have access to classified information, but national security laws prevent it from being disclosed directly to the public. The essence of that information can be understood if one accurately decodes the clues and infers the correct meaning from Q's questions. The reader ends up with a set of assumptions that convey information that would normally require a classified briefing.

Q's operation involves the exposure of corruption. His messages are read by both those who perpetrate crimes and those who attempt to expose it. Because Q's opponents read his messages, the strategies and tactics of game theory are used to keep them off guard and lure them into traps. Game theory involves the use of deception, distraction, disinformation, and bluffing.

For example, during the first week of November 2017, Q frequently promised that former Secretary of State Hillary Clinton, her campaign manager, John Podesta, and her personal assistant, Huma Abedin, would be arrested. During that week, these political figures were not arrested, but members of the Saudi royal family were. Q had also posted messages about Saudi Arabia that week but did not mention arrests. Is it possible that Q wanted attention to be focused on American political figures while arrests in Saudi Arabia were quietly being planned?

Q uses the Socratic method of instruction, which is a form of cooperative dialogue. The alternating asking and answering of questions encourages critical thinking, the analysis of ideas, and the examination of underlying presuppositions. Stronger hypotheses emerge by identifying and eliminating weaker ones. Q asks if our beliefs are logical, hints at facts we may not be aware of, and suggests alternative hypotheses.

Q claims to be closely connected to Donald Trump, but rather than confirming this relationship directly, it is done indirectly. For example, on many occasions, Q has posted a message 20 or 30 seconds before President Trump posted a tweet on his Twitter account. When Q is active, he posts about five times a day. President Trump tweeted about a dozen times a day before his Twitter account was suspended. The odds are small that they would coincidentally post at the same time, given that Q posts first. If it happened only once, it could be coincidental, but Q has posted before the President (within 60 seconds) on more than 30 occasions.

Before his account was suspended, the President often retweeted the Twitter accounts of people that follow Q. The mainstream media attacked Trump, claiming, on the one hand, that he was lending credibility to the Q movement, but on the other hand, insisting that he couldn't possibly be involved in the operation. Trump's retweets of Q promoters tacitly confirmed Q, but his retweets of Q's skeptics provided President Trump with plausible deniability.

Q intends to reveal as much information to the public as possible about hidden crime and corruption, but some subjects pose a risk if too much is said about them. Certain information, if it were to be released, could create serious conflict with allies of the United States, which could precipitate war and cause worldwide (WW in Q's vernacular) suffering.

Introduction

Q expressed this idea in this post:

> Feb 11, 2018
> Understand one simple fact - the US is connected to the rest of the world.
> Knowing that, understand, by default, if certain intel is released it would cause a WW/mass suffering. We share the idea of open source but value life and must make decisions base decisions on outcomes and containability.
> Q

In this book, when I refer to Q as "he" or "him," it is strictly for ease of writing. I do not know with certainty if Q is male, female, an individual, or a group. The consensus among researchers is that Q is a group comprised mostly of members of U.S. military intelligence.

Q originally posted on the 4chan board *politically incorrect* (sometimes called /pol/). 4chan users can remain anonymous, which is why government employees sometimes use it to post information about hidden government corruption. By day, anonymous users (also called anons or autists) work as systems analysts, coders, and game designers. By night, they research the clues posted (or *dropped*) on the board.

The presence of thousands of researchers was one reason Q initially posted on 4chan. Anons are excellent internet researchers. They've examined posts from intelligence community insiders (both real and fake) for years. Dealing with phonies makes them highly skeptical. Q's messages needed to be vetted for legitimacy. He knew that anons would scrutinize his posts, looking for flaws. If his messages could be verified, he would gain the trust of a group of hardened skeptics. Once his posts were verified, anons would become a conduit of information about the real stories behind world events and the actual facts of history that have been hidden from society.

Conversations on 4chan, 8chan, and 8kun are hosted on subdomains called *boards*. Each board hosts discussions on a particular topic. The boards are run by volunteers (board volunteers or BVs) who create and moderate conversations (threads). Board volunteers are sometimes called *bakers*. The threads are called *breads*. When a baker creates a new thread, they're said to be "baking a bread." A single comment in a thread is called a *crumb*. Helpful information on the topic is called *sauce*. The term sauce is derived from the word "source."

If a point is made that isn't common knowledge, others will ask for the source (sauce) of the information.

At present, Q communicates on two different boards hosted on 8kun. Messages on a read-only board can be viewed, but readers cannot leave comments. Posts that are intended for discussion are posted on a research board where anyone can comment.

Some people are shocked to find nudity when visiting 4chan, 8chan, and 8kun. Q does not post nudity, but some users of these forums do. Most people use social media platforms where nudity isn't allowed. The restriction against nudity is a form of censorship. Q anticipated that his posts would be controversial enough that they would be removed from mainstream platforms. To avoid censorship, Q chose to post on a forum where free speech (including nudity) is allowed.

Q has posted nearly 5,000 messages to date. Instead of covering every post, each volume in this series examines a sample of posts over a span of time and explores the main subjects discussed during that time period. This volume covers topics discussed between April and December of 2018. Whenever possible, details of those discussions will be examined from the time they were first mentioned until the present.

There are posts of every kind to be considered, including links to news articles, videos, and photographs. I'll provide information from news articles and videos when appropriate. I'll describe images to the best of my ability and provide commentary on them; however, copyright laws, privacy concerns, and space constraints make it impossible for the pictures themselves to be included in this book.

Many of Q's posts contain abbreviations, acronyms, or diagrams, as well as the initials of people and government agencies with which you may not be familiar. I've included a glossary at the back of the book to help explain them.

Please note that the formatting of Q's posts when they appear in this book will adhere to the following guidelines:

- If there were typos in a post by Q or an anon, the typos will also appear in this book. Note: Some of Q's "typos" are intentional and convey a message.

- In some cases, an original post by Q or an anon may contain blank lines between sections of text. We have tried as much as possible to preserve the original use of paragraph returns, but occasionally, they may be removed due to space constraints.

Introduction

- Dates will always be provided when I display a post by Q if they are relevant. I will occasionally break a long post into multiple sections and explain each part individually. In those cases, the date will appear at the top of the first section, but the sections that follow will not have a date because they're part of the same post.

- I will occasionally explain a conversation thread between two people that occurs on a single day. In those cases, the date of the first post will be displayed but the dates of the responses may be omitted.

- To limit distracting data, I've opted in most cases to omit the timestamps and user IDs from Q's posts. That information usually isn't relevant to the discussion. In the few cases where it is, timestamps and user IDs will be included.

- I've chosen, at times, to cut out certain parts of Q's posts while including other parts because, from a teaching standpoint, it's best if we focus on the part of the post that's relevant to the subject we're discussing. Some Q posts cover many topics, and it's easy to become confused or distracted by off-topic information. When I need to display only a section of a post, you'll see three diamonds like this: ♦♦♦ to indicate where part of the original message has been omitted.

CHAPTER 1

Ten Days Darkness

THERE HAS BEEN MUCH SPECULATION over the interpretation of several posts by Q that refer to "ten days darkness." In this chapter, we'll consider what those posts might mean.

On November 5th, 2017, Q posted the following message.

> Nov 5 2017
> Ten days.
> Darkness.
> Scare tactics (MSM).
> D's falling.
> R's walk-away/removed.
> SA --> US --> Asia --> EU
> Disinformation is real.
> Distractions are necessary.
> Focus was US today while real happening in SA under same context (military control, martial law, missile strike (rogue) etc).
> Necessary.
> POTUS' Twitter attack (see above).

> Important.
> Why is this relevant?
> What was the last Tweet by POTUS prior to SA?
> Why is this relevant?
> SA (1), US (2), Asia (3), EU (4).
> Where is POTUS?
> Why is this relevant?
> Military operations.
> Operators in US.
> Snow White
> The Great Awakening
> Godfather III
> Q

This message was posted just after members of the Saudi royal family were arrested on corruption charges. Q alluded to scare tactics being used by the mainstream media (MSM) and explained that distractions and disinformation are necessary. There was no clarification provided regarding the two statements: Ten days. Darkness. To this day, Q has not confirmed their meaning.

Another message was posted later the same day.

> Nov 5 2017
> Game Theory.
> Define.
> Why is this relevant?
> Moves and countermoves.
> Who is the enemy?
> False flags.
> Shooter identification.
> Shooter history.
> Shooter background.
> Shooter family.
> MS13.
> Define hostage.
> Define leverage.
> MS13.
> Shooter.

Family.
Hostage.
Force.
Narrative.
Race.
Background.
Why is this relevant?
Flynn.
What is Flynn's background?
What was his rank?
Was he involved in intel ops?
What access or special priv?
Why is this relevant?
Set up.
Who wins?
Who becomes exposed?
Who knows where the bodies are buried?
Who has access?
What is MI?
Who was part of MI during BO term?
Who was fired during BO term (MI)?
Why is this relevant?
Re-read complete crumb graphic (confirmed good).
Paint the picture.
Disinformation exists and is necessary.
10 days.
Darnkess.
War.
Good v. Evil.
Roadmap of big picture is here.
Review post happenings.
Clarified.
Crumbs not only for /pol/.
The silent ones.
Others monitoring (friends and enemies).
Instructions.
Snow White.
Godfather III.
Q

In this post, the number 10 was used instead of how it appeared in the previous post, where the word "ten" was spelled out. It's worth noting that the word "darkness" in the second post was misspelled "darnkess" and it was not corrected. I would also point out that just above the mention of 10 days darkness in the second post, information was given about the nature of the operation. Q encouraged followers to read the full graphic containing all of his posts, to "paint the picture"—or see the grand sweep of events playing out on the world stage. He also discussed the need for disinformation—a point that was mentioned in the first post. All of these things pertain to the manner in which Q constructs and posts his messages. They are, if you will, *operational considerations*—matters pertaining to the Q operation itself rather than the exposure of corruption. I believe "10 days darkness" is an operational consideration.

From his first post on October 28th through December 25th of 2017, the longest time Q went without posting was four days. I believe he wanted his followers to know that a longer interval without posts was coming. I suspect Q knew he was going to "go dark" for a length of time and did not want anons to worry.

The day after Q first mentioned ten days darkness, an anon asked when it would happen.

Anonymous • Dec 6 2017 21:01:21
I have a question: The 10 days, darkness.. when?

Q responded quickly as shown by the timestamp and suggested it had something to do with a shutdown.

Dec 6 2017 21:03:11
Shutdown.
Q

Some have assumed that the shutdown pertained to a power outage or interruption in internet service. A few have made predictions about such service interruptions, but none of these predictions have come to pass (at least not yet). It would be incredibly difficult for Q to correctly predict 10 days during which power or internet service would be interrupted since he would likely not have control over those services. In December of 2018, during a question-and-answer session, an anon asked Q how he is able to predict future events.

Anonymous • Dec 12 2018
How do you know the future?

Q responded.

> Control.
> Q

Q has knowledge of certain future events because he has some degree of control over them. But it seems unlikely he would have control over (or knowledge of) a widespread future power outage.

Q uses a hashed password called a tripcode to secure his identity on the board where he posts. On December 14th, 2017, Q told anons he could not enter his tripcode on the 8chan board /cbts/ and feared the board had been compromised.

> Dec 14 2017 21:20:48
> Blocked from posting entering 'trip'. It would appear this board has been compromised.
> Q

Forty minutes later, Q indicated he had lost access to the board due to his inability to enter a tripcode.

> Dec 14 2017 21:40:05
> Lost access to /cbts/
> No ability to enter trip code.
> Q

That message was followed by this one.

> Dec 14 2017 21:41:02
> ♦♦♦
> 24hrs to restore trip code or departure.
> Godspeed,
> Q

The following day, Q posted on the 8chan board /pol/ to advise anons that he was unable to post securely on the board /cbts/.

> Dec 15 2017 01:15:57
> We may have exhausted our ability to maintain safe-comms.
> Snow White.
> Rig for silent running.
> Unknown return.
> Godspeed, Patriots.
> Q

Thirteen minutes later, Q posted again.

> Dec 15 2017 01:28:58
> Follow the crumbs.
> You have it all.
> SEC Conf will be analyzed.
> Dark [10].
> Enjoy the show!
> Q

Q told anons to follow his posts (crumbs). He said that security configurations (SEC Conf) would be analyzed and wrote "Dark [10]." Given that he was experiencing problems with posting, it seems ten days of darkness pertained to a window of time when he would not post.

On December 25th, 2017, Q posted the following message.

> Dec 25 2017
> 10, [10-9]
> Operational_window(5-6)_FDeltaC25-26
> Secured.
> Floor is yours.
> Twitter FW_
> Twitter [kill_rogue]
> CONF_WHITE_WHITE_
> Q

This post began with the number 10 and contained what appeared to be the beginning of a countdown [10-9]. Q also mentioned an "operational window." We know from other posts that Q sometimes goes dark (does not post) during sensitive operations.

Ten days passed before Q posted his next message on January 4th, 2018.

> Jan 4 2018
> [J-Go_dX)-2-8
> Everything has meaning.
> Who is AMB Matlock?
> YES.
> /[RR-out][P_pers]
> EO_CLASSIFIED_WH[-6713A]
> SIG_con_MAR39sv3665BECD
> Q

It may not be as exciting as some had hoped for, but I believe "ten days darkness" was nothing more than a warning to anons that a period of ten days was coming when Q would not post. He would have control over such a time period, which would allow him to predict it in advance. That time period was from December 25th, 2017, through January 4th, 2018.

CHAPTER 2

Myths and Misconceptions about Q

AS Q'S POPULARITY HAS GROWN, some religious leaders have insisted that he leads people away from God. Members of the clergy have expressed several concerns. In this chapter, I'll address some of the more common ones.

An Illustration

The problem might best be illustrated through an analogy. I once met an atheist who said God doesn't exist. He claimed that this is what the Bible teaches. Intrigued by his statement, I asked him to explain. He replied, "The Bible says there is no God. Look it up in Deuteronomy chapter 32 and Isaiah 45." I examined the text of the verses he cited.

> "*See now that I, I am He,*
> *And there is no god besides Me;*
> *It is I who put to death and give life.*
> *I have wounded and it is I who heal,*
> *And there is no one who can deliver from My hand.*"
> -Deut. 32:39

"I am the Lord, and there is no other;
Besides Me there is no God.
I will gird you, though you have not known Me;
-Is. 45:5

My atheist friend was right. The Bible does say, "there is no God." But when we consider that phrase in context, we can see that in each case, it is part of a larger statement that emphasizes the realities of God's existence. When a statement is removed from its original context, it can be twisted to mean the opposite of what was intended.

The Context of Q

Q is an operation that provides information about historical and current events. The clues and information provided create a narrative of history different from the one disseminated by the mainstream media. This is the overarching context of Q's operation and it must be applied to all of Q's posts. If it is not—if Q's statements are taken out of context—they can be twisted to mean something other than their intended meaning. Sadly, that is what some people have done.

Sheep No More

One pastor took exception to Q's statement, "Sheep no more," which is found in the following post.

> Mar 28 2019
> ♦♦♦
> LOVE.
> UNITED NOT DIVIDED.
> SHEEP NO MORE.
> Q

In a sermon, the pastor rejoiced at the fact that Jesus called himself the Good Shepherd and referred to us as His sheep. He was outraged at the suggestion that we are not the Lord's sheep.

The comparison of humans to sheep is a metaphor that can be used to illustrate different ideas. It may describe, allegorically, the relationship between Jesus and His followers. We are called His sheep because sheep follow their shepherd. In this case, the allegory speaks of devotion. But the term can also be used in a derogatory way. Sheep are incredibly dumb animals. For that reason, people who are gullible and naive are often called sheep. In the context of Q's operation, those who blindly accept the mainstream media's narrative are referred to as sheep. In some cases, Q says the elites (who use occultic symbols to openly display their evil) see us as sheep.

> Nov 21 2017
> Their need for symbolism will be their downfall.
> Follow the Owl & Y head around the world.
> Identify and list.
> They don't hide it.
> They don't fear you.
> You are sheep to them.
> You are feeders.
> Godfather III.
> Q

Q has never suggested that we are not *God's* sheep. But when his statements are taken out of context, they can be twisted, and the argument is then made that he opposes the teaching of the Bible.

Trust Yourself

Some people are concerned about Q's admonition to "trust yourself."

> Aug 27 2018
> Think for yourself.
> Research for yourself.
> Trust yourself.
> Clickbait opinions are designed to attract reader to subscribe and/or follow and/or shape a pre-designed narrative.
> FOLLOW THE FACTS.
> SHEEP NO MORE.
> Q

Religious leaders have expressed concern that this goes against the biblical instruction to trust God. Once again, context is essential. We know that Q's operation is about uncovering the facts of historical and current events that are ignored or distorted by the mainstream media. In the post above, Q said news outlets report false information to receive clicks or to push a false narrative. Rather than blindly accepting their narrative, Q encourages us to do our own research and trust our conclusions. His statement "trust yourself" is an admonition to trust our understanding of current events after we conduct our own research rather than trusting the mainstream media. It has nothing to do with whether we trust God. It is God who helps me connect the details I uncover in my research. I depend on Him to give me understanding. In that regard, trusting yourself and trusting God are not antithetical.

The Savior of Mankind

One pastor objected to the fact that Q referred to the U.S. military as the "savior of mankind."

> Nov 5 2017
> US Military = savior of mankind.
> We will never forget.
> Fantasy land.
> God save us all.
> Q

The pastor launched into a diatribe before his congregation about how only God is our savior, and the idea that anyone else could be a savior is demonic.

If this statement is removed from its context, it can be twisted to mean something that was not intended. Q is not a theologian. His operation is not about religion. He does not normally teach on soteriology—how man's soul can be redeemed. Therefore, if he uses the term "savior" or "salvation," the intended reference would be to something other than theology.

In what other sense might the U.S. military be viewed as the savior of mankind?

Whether we choose to believe it or not, wealthy, powerful people procure children so they can be tortured and raped. Ghislaine Maxwell and Jeffrey Epstein were indicted for facilitating this kind of activity. Child sex trafficking isn't an isolated phenomenon; it happens in every country. Because civilian courts have often turned a blind eye to this problem, according to the Q post below, the U.S. military stepped in and began shutting down human trafficking lanes around the world.

> Aug 15 2018
> SA [ACCESS] CLOSED.
> EPSTEIN ISLAND [ACCESS] CLOSED.
> HAITI [ACCESS] CLOSED.
> NK [ACCESS] CLOSED.
> CHINA [ACCESS] CLOSED.
> RUSSA [ACCESS] CLOSED.
> CUBA [ACCESS] CLOSED.
> SUDAN [ACCESS] PENDING [GOV'T][SA US PUSH]
> SYRIA [ACCESS] PENDING [GOV'T]
> YEMEN [ACCESS] PENDING [GOV'T][SA US PUSH]
> LIBYA [ACCESS] PENDING [MAIN PORT CLOSED][LIMITED]
> SOMALIA [ACCESS] PENDING [SA US PUSH]
> Q

When Q says the U.S. military is the "savior of mankind," he means they are one of the only organizations in the world currently working to end the trafficking of those who cannot protect themselves. But even in the post where he supposedly committed blasphemy, Q closed with a statement his critics have ignored: "God save us all."

> Nov 5 2017
> US Military = savior of mankind.
> We will never forget.
> Fantasy land.
> God save us all.
> Q

I could provide more examples where someone took a Q post out of context and accused him of ungodly teaching, but hopefully, you get the point. If you find something in one of Q's posts that seems a bit off, before jumping to conclusions, consider the message within the context of Q's operation.

A religious leader may have an opinion about Q, but if they have not read Q's posts—or followed the decodes of someone who has—their opinion is uninformed. An uninformed opinion about any field of study is worth little, and Q is a massive field of study unto itself. In the same way that you can't understand microbiology without taking a class or reading a book on the subject, no life experience and no amount of education can give you an understanding of Q's operation. The only way to understand Q is to read the posts and do the required research. I respect the opinions of people who have expertise in certain areas, but there is no reason to respect the uninformed opinion of someone who hasn't bothered to read the posts.

Why Do People Worship Q?

It has been said that some people worship Q. That fact isn't surprising. Mankind was created to venerate (worship) God. It's encoded in our DNA; it's the purpose for which we were created. But not everyone sees the value in God. Some prefer to exalt Hollywood celebrities. Others kneel before the altar of their favorite NFL team. Still others find incredible value in the 17th letter of the alphabet. The fact that people choose to worship a person, an activity, or an idea, does not make the worshipped thing evil. When we choose to worship an idol, it says nothing about the idol, but it speaks volumes about us. Q has, on many occasions, cautioned people not to worship (glorify) the Q team.

> Jan 23 2018
> Do not glorify us.
> WE are ALL Patriots.
> Honor those who serve.
> FOR GOD, HUMANITY & COUNTRY.
> Where we go one, we go all.
> Q

Is Q a Cult?

While it is evident that Q followers are involved in some type of movement, to know if it is a cult, we need to know if the movement engages in the kind of behavior typically seen in cults. Most cults are centered around the teaching of a charismatic central figure who provides personal revelation and guidance to members. Cults generally have an established leadership hierarchy. The doctrines of the cult flow from the central figure to the leadership team and are reinforced by them. Cult followers are praised for learning and obeying the leader's teachings and observing the cult's rituals. They are punished or publicly humiliated when they don't.

There is a central figure in the Q movement, but no one knows who he (or she) is. The movement has no identified leaders. There are no official meetings that Q followers attend or even an organized way of communicating. There are no official (or even widely accepted) doctrines in the Q community. Each person who reads Q's posts finds their own meaning in them. They emphasize whatever ideas, values, or concepts are important to them. (Over time, consensus naturally develops on some issues.)

Cult leaders are primarily interested in controlling the thoughts and behaviors of members, while Q insists that people think for themselves. It may appear from a distance as though Q has recruited a cult following, but a close examination reveals this is not the case.

Some have claimed that although Q mentions God, he never mentions Jesus. In 2019, Q felt it was worth pointing out that Jesus Christ is the reason we celebrate Christmas.

Dec 17 2019
♦♦♦
Though, nothing should ever replace 'Christ' in 'Christmas'.
Merry Christmas, Anons/Patriots.
God is on our side.
Q

CHAPTER 3

Iron Eagle

Q SOMETIMES CLOSES A POST with a short phrase that represents a topic discussed in that post. These phrases are called *signatures*.

> Nov 5 2017
> My signatures all reference upcoming events about to drop if this hasn't been caught on.
> Snow White
> Godfather III
> Q

Signatures serve as warnings of coming events. Many are the titles of films. Understanding a film's plot will tell you something about the posts that contain that signature. In this chapter, we'll explore the signature "Iron Eagle."

Iron Eagle was a 1986 film featuring Lou Gossett Jr. as Chappy, an aging military pilot who befriended a teenager named Doug Masters, who aspired to become a fighter pilot. Doug's father, Ted, was a fighter pilot stationed at the same airbase as Chappy. While flying a mission over an unfriendly middle eastern nation, Ted's plane was shot down. He was captured and sentenced to death. When the U.S. government failed to take action to help Ted, his son Doug convinced Chappy to accompany him on a rescue mission. They stole a pair of F-16 fighter jets, flew to the middle east, and effected a rescue.

To summarize: An unconventional operation against a rogue middle eastern nation gave American patriots a victory. If we assume there is a real-life event that mimics the film's storyline, to decode the signature "Iron Eagle," we may want to know the name of the rogue nation and the name of the operation.

On December 7th, 2017, Q explained that a handful of influential people control global events.

Dec 7 2017
Rothschilds (cult leaders)(church)(P)
Banks / Financial Institutions
WW Gov Control
Gov Controls People
SA
Oil Tech Sex/Children
SA Controls (assigned) US / UK Politicians / Tech Co's (primary)
Soros
Controls organizations of people (create division / brainwash) + management / operator of slush funds (personal net worth never reduces think DOJ settlements Consumer Iran Enviro pacts etc etc)
/_\ - Rock (past)(auth over followers)
_\ (present)
(Future)
Order is critical.
Strings cut to US/UK.
Expand your thinking.
♦♦♦
Q

Using the shape of a triangle, Q illustrated the wealth, power, and worldwide (WW) influence of a small group of people. One side of the triangle represents the Saudi royal family, one side represents the Rothschild banking family, and the third side, George Soros. According to Q, each plays a part in controlling the geopolitical landscape. The Rothschilds primarily control banks and financial institutions and, through them, national governments and the church. By controlling governments and the church, they control large numbers of people.

According to Q, Saudi Arabia has maintained economic control via its oil reserves, and it has exerted control over some U.S. and U.K. politicians through pedophilia and blackmail. Saudi princes like Al Waleed bin Talal have been major investors in the tech sector and the media, including social media platforms.

George Soros funds far left political activists and progressive organizations. Q has suggested that slush funds (like the Department of Justice Settlements fund) have been set up by politicians to take taxpayer money and re-route it to fund Soros organizations, which provide propaganda to keep people unaware and confused.

Q indicated that the triangular-shaped diagram—illustrating the power structure of the Saudi royal family, George Soros, and the Rothschilds—has changed. Following the arrest of members of the Saudi royal family in 2017 and the ascension of moderate Mohammad bin Salman, one side of the power triangle was removed. Its removal cut the strings of control the Saudis had over many U.S. and U.K. politicians.

A similar message was conveyed in the following post, which contains the signature "Iron Eagle."

Nov 11 2017
Wealth (over generations) buys power.
Power (over generations) buys more wealth/control.
More wealth/control buys countries and its people.
Families combined (TRI) = NWO.
Inner TRI families will collapse.
What is the keystone?
What Nation dominates all others?
What Nation has influence over most others?
What is the keystone?
Return to SA.
Strings cut (+++).
Puppets (+++) in shadows.
Each side of the triangle controls a certain subsect of power brokers.
Power brokers are also labeled as the puppets/servants.

What is the New World Order?
Why did POTUS receive a sword dance when visiting SA?
What does this mean culturally?
Why is this relevant?
What occurred in SA?
How did POTUS remove one side of the pyramid?
What did POTUS receive while visiting China?
Where did POTUS dine?
What is the significance?
What if China, Russia, and others are coordinating w/ POTUS to eliminate the NWO?
Who controls NK?
Who really controls NK?
Who controls several agencies within the US, EU, and abroad?
Why is No Such Agency so vital?
Enormous scale of events currently ongoing.
Why is Russia helping to kill ISIS?
This is not easy to accept nor believe.
Crumbs make bread.
Operations active.
Joint missions underway.
The world is fighting back.
Refer back to graphic.
The Great Awakening.
Snow White.
Iron Eagle.
Jason Bourne (2016)(Dream/CIA).
Q

Q explained that wealth and power are consolidated over time to create more wealth and power. The New World Order was established by the Rothschilds, the Saudi royal family, and George Soros. Q wrote:

What Nation dominates all others?
What Nation has influence over most others?
What is the keystone?
Return to SA.
Strings cut (+++).
Puppets (+++) in shadows.

According to Q, Saudi Arabia (SA) exerted power over most nations. When members of the royal family were arrested on November 4th, 2017, their power was removed and, metaphorically, the strings they used to control politicians were cut.

In January of 2018, an anon asked Q about Saudi Prince Al Waleed bin Talal's finances.

> **Anonymous** • Jan 14 2018
> just saw story about alwaleed in prison because he won't pay 6 billion to secure freedom

Q responded.

> He doesn't have 6b.
> We froze his assets.
> Think logically.
> When does a BIRD TALK?
> Q

Executive Order 13818, signed by President Trump on December 20th, 2017, authorized the Treasury Department to seize the assets of people and organizations involved in corruption, human rights abuse, and human trafficking. Al Waleed bin Talal was one of the people whose assets were frozen as a result of the Executive Order.

On December 5th, 2017, Q began to explain the keystone.

> Dec 5 2017 16:01:30
> Key - unlocks the door of all doors (info)
> Stone - the force / strength capable of yielding power to act on info
> Key+Stone=
> Q

Q's keystone is comprised of two parts. The "key" is information. Metaphorically, it opens the door to unknown things. Q also called information the "door of all doors." The "stone" is the strength or power to act on information. Five minutes after the above post, Q provided more clues about the keystone.

Dec 5 2017 16:06:17
Adm R/ No Such Agency (W&W) + POTUS/USMIL =
Apply the Keystone.
Paint the picture.

The former director of the National Security Agency (No Such Agency) was Admiral Mike Rogers. Q occasionally refers to "the council of wizards and warlocks." In the above post, the abbreviation W&W is a reference to that idea. On December 12th, 2017, an anon asked who the Wizards and Warlocks were.

Anonymous • Dec 12 2018
Q, please tell us who or what the Wizards and Warlocks are.

Q replied.

'Guardians' of intelligence.
Q

On December 5th, Q reposted a message by an anon, confirming that he had the correct decode for Keystone.

Anonymous • Dec 5 2017
Military Intelligence, No Such Agency = key
POTUS and Patriots = stone

Intelligence collected by the National Security Agency is the "key." The power of the office of the President combined with the might of the U.S. military and the networking capabilities of patriots is the "stone." When combined, they form the "keystone."

Information provided by the military helps us understand events that are happening on the world stage (revealing the big picture). Researchers around the globe help the military and President Trump by disseminating the information they provide.

The following post covers many subjects, which will be discussed below. Note that the post closes with four signatures, one of which is Iron Eagle.

Nov 20 2017
What is a key?

What is a key used for?
What is a guard?
What is a guard used for?
Who unlocked the door of all doors?
Was it pre-planned?
Do you believe in coincidences?
What is information?
Who controls the release of information?
WHO HAS ALL OF THE INFORMATION?
Who disseminates information?
What is the MSM?
Who controls the MSM?
Who really controls the MSM?
Why are we made to believe the MSM are the only credible news sources?
Who controls the MSM?
Who really controls the MSM?
Why are we made to believe the MSM are the only credible news sources?
Why is this relevant?
Why are non MSM platforms cast as conspiracy and/or non-credible?
Why are non MSM platforms cast as conspiracy and/or non-credible?
What happens when an entity and/or individual accumulates power?
Define corruption.
Wealth = power.
Power = influence.
Influence = control.
Rinse and repeat.
What power of influence was recently discovered (specifically re: 2016 election)?
How much power of influence does Twitter, FB, Reddit, etc. have in influencing the minds of people?
Has the stranglehold of the MSM been diminished?
What is open source?
What has become blatantly obvious since the election of POTUS?

Why would they allow this (visibility) to occur?
Were they not prepared to counter?
What miscalculation occurred?
What opposite impact did this generate?
How did POTUS recognize and invert?
What happens when an entity and/or individual accumulates power?
Define corruption.
Define censorship.
Define 'controlled' censorship.
What action is Twitter taking effective mid-Dec?
What is the purpose of this action?
Possible test to understand public / gov't response?

Nov 20 2017
(cont..)
When was this announced?
When did events in SA transpire?
Who controlled a large portion of Twitter stock?
Why is this relevant?
Define oppression.
Who controls the narrative?
Who really controls the narrative?
Who guards the narrative?
Does the MSM shelter and protect select 'party' members?
Does this protection insulate these 'party' members?
Who controls the narrative?
What laws were put in place to protect the MSM from lawsuits?
Who specifically passed this law?
What is immunity?
What prevents a news organization from simply 'making up sources & stories'?
What prevents a news organization from simply 'making up sources & stories'?
What previous SC ruling provided protection to reporters from having to reveal their 'confidential' source(s)?
How many people are unaware of the 'truth' due to the stranglehold?
How must people be made aware of an alternate reality?

What are crumbs (think H-wood/DC)
Define 'lead-in' (think play)?
What has been occurring recently?
The stage must be set.
Crumbs are easy to swallow.
What if Hugh Hefner was /a Clown In America?
What is a honeypot?
Define blackmail.
How could this be applied?
Fantasy land.
WHO HAS ALL OF THE INFORMATION?
No Such Agency.
The hunter becomes the hunted.
Operations underway.
Operators active.
Disinformation is real.
Disinformation is necessary.
Silent war (some gets out).
The Great Awakening.
Iron Eagle.
Godfather III.
The Hunt for Red October.
Q

The open source information provided by Q can be thought of metaphorically as a key that opens doors which conceal certain things. Q suggested that President Trump opened the "door of all doors." This speaks of a vast amount of information being released that will cause major changes on the geopolitical stage. President Trump released some of that open source information through Q.

Q uses the word "crumb" to denote at least two different ideas. Anons who conduct research on boards like 4chan and 8kun refer to messages posted on a board as "crumbs." But in the post above, the word is used to describe a safe path out of the false reality created by the media and into a more realistic view of the world.

Q suggested that a corrupt agency controls the mainstream media. In a 1977 article published in *The Rolling Stone*, Carl Bernstein claimed that more than 400 fellow reporters were working for the CIA. Q implied that deceased playboy tycoon Hugh Hefner was a CIA asset who provided a location for powerful people to have illicit sex and secretly videotaped the encounters so the CIA could use them as blackmail.

During the 20th century, the mainstream press (and indirectly, the CIA) maintained control of the information on which ordinary people relied. This information dominance allowed them to choose narratives and opinions they could emphasize or downplay through radio, television, and print media. Today, most people turn to social media platforms like Facebook, Twitter, and YouTube for quick news updates. Al Waleed bin Talal owned a controlling interest in Twitter and some broadcast networks, but the asset freeze in 2017, weakened that control.

Q pointed out that social media platforms were supposed to prevent Trump from being elected in 2016, but their CEOs underestimated the influence people exert when they collectively speak their minds. Trump supporters countered the mainstream narrative, giving him a victory in 2016. Then, realizing their mistake, social media companies silenced dissenters. Censorship has increased, and many conservatives have had their social media accounts canceled. Silicon Valley CEOs justify their actions against debate and discussion by labeling dissenting opinions "hate speech" or "disinformation." Q suggested that to help control the narrative, Congress enacted laws protecting the media from litigation and from disclosing their sources. Even members of Congress may leak damaging (sometimes false) information to the press without worrying about accountability.

On February 7th, 2018, Q posted the following message.

>Feb 7 2018
>You have so much more than you know.
>SO MUCH!
>Future proves past.
>News unlocks map.
>=
>+
>++
>+++
>RED OCTOBER.
>IRON EAGLE.
>[]
>Q

Q provides information in a way that conceals its full relevance when it is posted. As news stories are published and we look back at previous posts, we find clues about current events hidden in messages posted weeks or months earlier. The "map" is a compilation of all of Q's posts. News stories unlock their meaning. Because their meaning is, in a sense, locked until a news story can be connected to it, we have far more information than we realize.

The above post included the plus signs (+, ++, +++) that pertain to George Soros (+), the Rothschilds (++), and the House of Saud (+++) as indicated in the post below.

> Nov 11 2017
> Hard to swallow.
> Important to progress.
> Who are the puppet masters?
> House of Saud (6+++) - $4 Trillion+
> Rothschild (6++) - $2 Trillion+
> Soros (6+) - $1 Trillion+
> Focus on above (3).
> Public wealth disclosures – False.
> ♦♦♦
> Q

The February 7th post closes with the signatures Red October and Iron Eagle and has a set of square brackets. Upon seeing the brackets, anons wondered what they signified.

> **Anonymous** • Feb 7 2018 18:57:55
> military target square?

Q replied.

> Kill box.
> Q

As used by the military, a kill box is a target area that aids joint weapons fire. Using a kill box, assets deployed can engage a surface target without further coordination or confirmation. In a Q post, when someone's name appears within brackets (kill box), it means action or focus on them can be expected in the near future. That action is non-violent and not usually specified by Q. In this context, the kill box is simply a metaphor.

On February 18th, 2018, Q posted a quote from President Trump.

> Feb 18 2018
> "Never gotten over the fact that Obama was able to send $1.7 Billion Dollars in CASH to Iran and nobody in Congress, the FBI or Justice called for an investigation!"
> Re_read crumbs.
> What is the reason this is being brought back up?
> There is a purpose for every tweet and crumb dropped.
> Follow the money.
> Future proves past.
> The Great Awakening.
> NO ESCAPE.
> NO DEALS.
> TRUST THE PLAN.
> HAPPY SUNDAY.
> Q

A frequent topic mentioned by Q is the Joint Comprehensive Plan of Action (JCPOA), more commonly known as the "Iran deal." The Iran deal is relevant to this discussion, so I'll provide a summary of it.

In April of 2006, Iran's president announced that they had enriched uranium for the first time. Two months later, on June 6th, 2006, China, France, Germany, Russia, the United Kingdom, and the United States offered Iran incentives for halting its uranium enrichment program. Iran rejected the proposal. Later that year, sanctions were levied against Iran.

Nine years later, in October 2015, Iran signed an agreement known as the Joint Comprehensive Plan of Action (JCPOA). However, the plan would not be implemented until Iran made changes to its uranium enrichment program. In addition, the changes would need to be verified by the International Atomic Energy Agency (IAEA). On January 16th, 2016, the IAEA verified that Iran had met its commitments. Based on the IAEA's report, implementation began, and sanctions were lifted.

On the following day, January 17th, 2016, the Obama State Department announced it had agreed to pay Iran $1.7 billion to settle a case related to the sale of military equipment prior to the 1979 Iranian revolution.

During the 38-year reign of the shah, Iran was one of the United States' closest allies in the Middle East and purchased billions of dollars' worth of U.S. arms. Weeks before its regime fell in 1979, Iran signed a new military agreement with the Carter administration valued at $400 million. American companies never delivered the weapons because of the Islamic revolution. That $400 million was frozen along with the suspension of diplomatic relations. Iran's claim to recapture the money had been tied up at the Hague Tribunal since 1981. The Obama administration said it was returning the principal money invested in the fund along with $1.3 billion in owed interest. In addition to the $1.7 billion repayment, Obama authorized the release of approximately $150 billion in previously frozen assets.

In the following post, Q asked several questions about the Iran deal.

Aug 28 2018
♦♦♦
How were the pallets of cash divided?
How many planes were used to transport?
Who operated the planes?
What 'shadow' agency directed operations?
Why wasn't the money [simply] wire transferred?
US had AUTH to open bank-to-bank transfers.
How do you prevent financial T logs?
How were the cash withdrawals in EU categorized/labeled?
Where did the cash originate from?
What time of day did the withdrawals occur?
Who provided SECURITY?
Why wasn't Congress notified?
Why was the U.S. Gov't kept in the DARK?
US law broken?
Did ALL planes land in the same location (airport)?
Why did [1] particular plane land outside of Iran?
Why was a helicopter involved?
[WHO] did the money go to?
HOW DO YOU AUDIT A FOREIGN AID BIG BLOCK TRANSFER?
Did Rouhani keep 'unknown' comms as insurance?
What agency did @Snowden work for orig?
Did he train on THE FARM?

When did @Snowden join No Such Agency?
Define 'Contractor'.
Define the 'PRISM' program.
What year did @Snowden release spec-details of PRISM?
Mid 2013?
IMPACT-LIMIT NSA's ability to utilize/collect?
FAKE NEWS push for Congressional restrictions?
OPEN SOURCE PUSH to create COUNTER-DEF?
PURPOSE?
BLUE SKIES FOR CLOWN OP?
When was the Joint Plan of Action (IRAN DEAL) executed?
Late 2013?
Do you believe in coincidences?
Nothing to See Here.
Q

At the time of the transfer of money to Iran, the Obama administration insisted the payment of cash and the release of previously frozen funds was not related to the implementation of the Iran deal, but later admitted it was an incentive to complete the deal.

According to an August 3rd, 2016, article by Jay Solomon of *The Wall Street Journal*, the Obama administration secretly coordinated an airlift of $400 million in cash to Iran. The payment of cash coincided with the release of four Americans who had been detained in Tehran. In return, the U.S. released seven Iranian nationals who were either jailed in the U.S. or facing charges.

The entire $1.7 billion was wired from the U.S. to the central banks of the Netherlands and Switzerland. The Obama administration said this arrangement was necessary because Iran did not have access to normal banking transactions due to sanctions. News reports have only described the transfer of $400 million in cash to Iran without reporting on what happened to the other $1.3 billion. *The Wall Street Journal* first reported that $400 million in cash was withdrawn in Swiss francs, Euros, and other currencies, then flown from Geneva to Iran on pallets in an unmarked cargo plane.

On August 24th, 2016, an article by *Fox News* provided information about the remaining $1.3 billion. State Department spokeswoman Elizabeth Trudeau said the U.S. government sent the wire transfers as 13 separate payments of $99,999,999.99 each and a final payment of $10 million.

One Obama official said the $1.3 billion was converted to cash and disbursed to a representative of Iran's central bank. However, the U.S. Treasury, Justice, and State Department officials refused to cooperate with a Congressional investigation into the matter. When questioned by *The Washington Free Beacon,* a State Department official said they did not know how or to whom the $1.3 billion was transferred.

Q suggested the wire transfers and conversion to cash were done *not* because Iran couldn't receive direct payment due to sanctions—as Obama had claimed—but because the details of the transactions had to be concealed since laws had been broken.

The Obama administration concealed the details of the money transfer, and then after some time had passed, they disclosed how $400 million was transferred to Iran. Rather than being *sent* to Iran, it seems the $1.3 billion was converted to cash and transferred via several aircraft to different locations.

Q asked what "shadow" agency directed the operations. An article by Jay Solomon of *The Wall Street Journal* on August 3rd, 2016, confirmed that the CIA and FBI were, at a minimum, involved in the prisoner exchange aspect of the deal, having met in Geneva with Iranian intelligence operatives in November and December of 2016.

♦♦♦
Did ALL planes land in the same location (airport)?
Why did [1] particular plane land outside of Iran?
Why was a helicopter involved?
[WHO] did the money go to?
HOW DO YOU AUDIT A FOREIGN AID BIG BLOCK TRANSFER?
♦♦♦

On May 8th, 2018, President Trump announced that the U.S. was withdrawing its support for the JCPOA and imposing sanctions on Iran. On May 12th, Q provided more information about the Iran deal, including how many aircraft were used to transport the money and how many routes were taken to deliver it.

May 12 2018
Re_read crumbs re: Iran.
It was never about WW safety & security.
It was never about Nuclear disarmament.

It was about opening a new untapped market.
It was about securing a black site.
The 'Exchange'.
U1.
Risk the welfare of the world.
Why?
Money.
Organized/planned by BC/HRC.
Carried out by Hussein.
[remember HRC ran against Hussein]
U1 [donations to CF].
$1.7b in-cash transfer to Iran [4 routes][5 planes].
Did the total withdrawal actually depart EU?
Why EU?
Define bribe.
Define kickback.
Special Interest Groups (SIG).
What US/EU Co's Immediately closed large deals in Iran post deal? https://www.nytimes.com/2018/05/09/business/iran-nuclear-trump-business-europe.html
Cross check Co's against political + foundation payments.
Define bribe.
Define kickback.
Why are people panicking about Iran deal pullout?
THEY NEVER THOUGHT SHE WOULD LOSE.
Truth coming.
Q

According to Q, most of the money from the Iran deal was never intended to reach Iran. It was wired to European central banks because the recipients were European leaders. The $1.3 billion was converted to cash, then given to them in exchange for their cooperation and silence. Five airplanes delivered the money to four destinations. (In the previous post, Q also said one helicopter was used.)

U.S. and European companies closed lucrative deals with Iranians soon after the Iran deal was announced. The linked article Q posted explained that automakers like Daimler and PSA Peugeot Citroën signed contracts with Iranian companies to sell vehicles. Siemens of Germany signed a deal to deliver locomotives. Total of France began an offshore natural gas exploration project. Q implied in this post that some of those companies made contributions to the Clinton Foundation. It seems that the scheme was hatched by Bill and Hillary Clinton (BC/HRC) and executed by Obama. They didn't expect Hillary Clinton to lose the 2016 election; therefore, they did not fear being exposed and took actions that put the safety of the world at risk.

On April 21st, 2018, Q hinted about an event for the following week.

> Apr 21 2018
> What will next week hold?
> MOAB.
> Q

Q responded to his previous post.

> Fire up those Memes!
> Please stand by.
> On the clock.
> Ready to play?
> MOAB incoming.
> Q

Anons were instructed by Q to prepare memes and be ready. MOAB is an acronym for mother of all bombs. "On the clock" suggests that a major event was imminent.

On April 24th, 2018, President Trump met with French President Emmanuel Macron. Three days later, he met with German Chancellor Angela Merkel. Anons wondered about their intentions.

> **Anonymous** • Apr 24 2018
> Q, is Macron a true ally to POTUS?

Q replied.

> His sole purpose [WH visit] is to convince POTUS, on behalf of the EU, to remain in the Iran deal.
> You decide.
> Q

The objective of the meetings with Merkel and Macron was to keep the U.S. in the Iran deal, which wasn't about nuclear disarmament but securing a site for the covert development of nuclear weapons.

One day before President Trump met with Macron, Q posted this list of statements and questions.

> Apr 23 2018 12:56:57
> Reminder.
> Iran is next.
> Marker.
> CLAS - Sec 11A P 2.2.
> "Installments."
> $250B.
> Jan 1.
> Jun 1.
> No inspection @ GZ NR sites.
> No missile tech prevention.
> Load carrying.
> ICBM.
> Think NK.
> Who controls the $?
> Who really controls the $?
> Why does the EU have a vested interest in this deal?
> Who receives the money?
> When the US sends billions in aid and/or climate and/or etc who or what entity audits / tracks to confirm intended recipient(s) rec?
> None.
> How does GS fund WW counter-events?
> Who funds WW leftist events?
> American taxpayer (subsidize).
> Define nuclear stand-off.
> Who benefits?
> How do you 'squeeze' funds out of the US?
> Threat to humanity?
> Environment push?
> Think Paris accord.
> Who audits / tracks the funneled money?
> Define kickback.

Define slush fund.
EPA.
No oversight re: Hussein.
Why?
How does the C_A fund non sanctioned ops?
Off the books?
Re_ read past drops.
Will become relevant.
Welcome Mr. President.
The U.S. will NOT agree to continue the Iran deal as it currently stands.
Q

Q said there was no provision in the Iran deal to conduct legitimate inspections of nuclear sites, and nothing would prevent Iran from developing missile technology. In addition to cash received at the time of the Iran deal, Q suggested politicians also expected to receive bi-annual payments of $250 billion. If true, it would provide a hefty incentive to remain in the deal.

He added that many causes that are promoted as necessary to save the world, such as the Paris Climate Accord and aid to foreign governments, are, in fact, scams that funnel taxpayer money to politicians. People support the taxes and fees, thinking that the money is being spent on a worthy cause. President Trump understood that many of these causes are scams, which is why he opposed them. Apparently, these transactions are not audited. Taxpayer money diverted to slush funds pays for off-the-books CIA operations. Q reminded anons that Iran was next.

Less than an hour later, Q posted a link to an article explaining that Armenia was going to hold snap elections after protests against corrupt leaders came to a head.

Apr 23 2018 13:48:13
Do you believe?
The world is awakening.
https://www.aljazeera.com/amp/news/2018/04/armenia-prime-minister-serzh-sargsyan-resigns-protests-180423120123655.html?__twitter_impression=true
Coincidence?
Q

Three minutes later, Q posted again.

> Apr 23 2018 13:51:38
> Why was Armenia mentioned recently?
> Clowns losing control.
> Q

A week earlier, Q mentioned Armenia and said four unique user IDs operating as CIA assets were currently on the board. He also mentioned that searches for 'qanon' were ranked at the top in Armenia.

> Apr 15 2018
> [4] Clown UIDs here.
> Armenia.
> GOOG 'qanon' search stats (by country).
> Armenia #1.
> Q

On April 23rd, Q said that just as the CIA's control of North Korea had ended, their influence in Armenia was also removed.

> Apr 23 2018 14:19:33
> Like NK, they have been freed.
> Assets on the ground.
> Q

Q explained that a specific order of operations was planned for freeing countries from the CIA's control.

> Apr 23 2018 14:31:49
> Think SA.
> Order is important.
> SA -> NK.
> NK -> Armenia.
> Armenia -> Iran
> Iran ->
> Any other rogue nuclear states?
> Define hostage.
> Define protection.

Who is protected by rogue nuclear states?
Trust the plan.
THE WORLD IS CONNECTED.
Why are border states like AZ/CA important?
Why is MX vocal against POTUS?
Those who are the loudest......
WWG1WGA.
The Great Awakening.
Iron Eagle.
Q

First, the CIA's influence was removed in Saudi Arabia. Then it was removed in North Korea, and Armenia. As of this writing, CIA influence has not yet been removed from other nations, but Q says it will be soon. Border states like Arizona and California are important because the end game for globalists is eradicating international borders and creating a global superstate. Globalists currently use borders to infiltrate nations with foreigners, changing the demographic population. Over time, this erases national identity and brings more voters to support the globalist agenda. In addition, weak borders invite trafficking of humans, drugs, and guns.

President Trump's decision to withdraw from the JCPOA angered Iran's leaders, who immediately threatened to increase their uranium enrichment. The following day, April 24th, 2018, President Trump said if Iran continued its nuclear weapons program, it would have bigger problems than ever before.

In response, Q posted this.

> Apr 24 2018 10:27:03 (EST)
> Iran is next.
> [Marker].
> Re_read.
> POTUS today.
> "Mark it down."
> "Bigger problems than ever before."
> SIG to Iran?
> CLAS - Sec 11A P 2.2 [important]
> Refers to more than continued payments of $250B.

IRON EAGLE.
Sweet Dreams.
Q

An anon asked when the MOAB (mother of all bombs) was coming.

Anonymous • Apr 24 2018
When will we have MOAB?

Q replied.

Should we tell all the good people watching the day & time?
Red carpet rollout?
Think logically.
The world is watching.
Q

It would be foolhardy to tell the world the day and time of the big event since it would tip off bad actors. For that reason, Q doesn't broadcast the dates of major events. Instead, false dates are sometimes given to force enemies to make wrong moves.

Five days later, on April 29th, Q posted a link to a tweet by the U.S. Embassy in Jordan's Twitter account, welcoming Secretary of State Mike Pompeo to the country.

Apr 29 2018 23:26:09
https://mobile.twitter.com/USEmbassyJordan/
status/990666003037204481
Q

Here is the text of the tweet.

U.S. Embassy Jordan (from their Twitter account):
اهلا وسهلا بوزير الخارجية الامريكي مايك بومبيو في #الاردن
Welcome to Jordan Secretary of State Mike Pompeo #usainjo
11:55 AM - 29 Apr 2018

Four minutes later, Q posted a link to a tweet by the U.S. Department of Defense Twitter account and hinted that the two tweets were connected.

Apr 29 2018 23:32:02
Connect.
No coincidences.
https://mobile.twitter.com/DeptofDefense/status/990772726884392965
Q

Here is the text of the Defense Department tweet.

Department of Defense (from their Twitter account):
Here comes the boom! 💥
@USMC
#Marines brace while an entrance is breached during exercise #EagerLion18 in #Jordan
7:00 PM - 29 Apr 2018

On the following day, April 30th, 2018, Israel's then-Prime Minister, Benjamin Netanyahu, held a news conference where he provided evidence that Iranian leaders had lied about their nuclear weapons program. He explained that Israeli intelligence operatives had uncovered evidence that Iran had built secret nuclear weapons facilities in Iran and Syria.

Q responded to the announcement.

Apr 30 2018
Knowing what you know now.
re: Israel disclosure moments ago.
Authentic.
Why is Sec of State there?
WHY IS THE EU / OTHERS PRESSING TO REMAIN IN THE DEAL?
Think logically.
France & Germany came to the WH for the sole purpose of pressing POTUS to remain in the deal.
5% shared.
POTUS deCLAS Syria/Iran + U1 connection.
Where does EU fit in?
SICK!
Q

Netanyahu's disclosure happened to coincide with NATO's annual two-week live-fire exercise in Jordan, called Eager Lion. Did patriots plan Netanyahu's disclosure to coincide with a military exercise in which friendly firepower in the region would be increased without alarming their enemies?

Joint Exercise Eager Lion solves the riddle of the signature we've studied in this chapter. Eager Lion is an anagram for Iron Eagle, a signature that first appeared in Q's posts in November of 2017.

Although Q didn't overtly confirm the day of the MOAB when he was first asked about it, in hindsight, we can see that he *did* provide the exact day. It just so happens that the Emmy awards, a red-carpet event, was held on April 30th, the day Netanyahu made his announcement.

> Apr 30 2018
> Emmy awards.
> Red carpet event?
> Q

CHAPTER 4

Sparrow Red

A CHEMICAL ATTACK WAS CARRIED out in the city of Douma, Syria on April 7th, 2018. According to reports, two Syrian Air Force Mi-8 helicopters released barrel bombs containing chlorine and the nerve agent sarin, killing more than 70 people. President Trump and his NATO allies blamed Syrian President Bashar al Assad for this attack and condemned it, later noting that it violated the Syrian regime's "obligations under international law, the Chemical Weapons Convention, and several United Nations Security Council Resolutions, including Security Council Resolution 2118". Syria's allies, Iran and Russia, denied that chemical weapons were used. In this chapter, we will examine posts by Q related to those events.

On April 4th, 2018, three days *before* the chemical attack, Q indicated that President Trump would be awake that night.

Apr 4 2018 20:45:45 (EST)
POTUS will be up all night.
Pray.
Watch the news tomorrow.
Q

Just after midnight that same evening, Q+ posted this message.

> Apr 5 2018 00:10:03 (EST)
> 5:5
> Q+

Aviators rate radio transmissions for clarity and signal strength on a scale from one to five, with one being poor and five being good. 5:5 means a message is loud and clear, or in Q's vernacular—it is understood. It is believed that messages signed by Q+ are sent by President Trump.

Approximately 22 hours later, Q posted the following message.

> Apr 5 2018 22:35:21 (EST)
> Thank you for your prayers.
> Forced reaction.
> One of many vehicles.
> Intercepts.
> Night [2]
> Birds.
> Fast movers.
> Force projection.
> April Showers.
> Q

It seems the U.S. military's operation in the middle east had forced an opponent to react. Fast-moving aircraft (birds) were involved. Force projection is a nation's ability to deploy and sustain military operations outside its borders. Q indicated that April 5th was night two, but it is unclear what exactly that meant.

Less than three hours later, Q posted the following message.

> Apr 6 2018 01:16:37 (EST)
> BOOMs en route.
> Blind.
> 5:5
> GREEN_578cDT324-45785sd4DMP
> Q

BOOMs can mean many things, but in light of an ongoing military operation, I would assume this message pertained to the delivery of an explosive ordnance. Q often uses "green" to indicate that an action has been authorized or given a "green light."

Four minutes later, Q posted again.

> Apr 6 2018 01:20:00
> Device hold.
> Comms transfer castle.
> Chatter.
> Rig for silent.
> Q+

When a sensitive military operation is underway, Q sometimes notes that operators must rig for silent running. Communications were transferred to the White House, which is often referred to as the castle. Once again, the post was signed by Q+.

Two days later, on April 8th, the day after the chemical attack in Douma, Q posted the following message.

> Apr 8 2018 00:09:53 (EST)
> Night [4]
> Increase in chatter.
> Auth B19-2.
> Sparrow Red.
> Prevent at all costs.
> Good.
> Castle_Online.
> Q

Knowing that this message was sent while military operations were ongoing in the middle east, we can infer that there was an increase in communications (chatter) by certain people, perhaps enemies of the United States. Q indicated that something referred to as B19-2 had been authorized, and it seemed to be related to Sparrow Red. If we assume this message pertained to a military campaign, the word sparrow could refer to a missile since sparrow is a type of missile. The operational goal seems to have been to prevent the escalation of war at all costs. I would infer that "Good" was a reference to the quality of intelligence upon which the operation was based. The White House (castle) was online; it was being kept up to date on events as they played out. April 8th was night [4].

Six minutes later, Q posted again.

> Apr 8 2018 00:15:40 (EST)
> Prevent.
> Auth 1st S.
> Castle_Green.
> FRhYd5894-3580-357DBECg
> Contact window ok.
> Q

My interpretation of this post is that a first strike was authorized with the goal of preventing the escalation of the larger conflict. The White House (castle) had given the operation the green light, and the contact window was okay. Sometimes, posts contain coded stringers (FRhYd5894-3580-357DBECg) that are intended for operators in the field. These stringers do not need to be decoded by anons.

Nine minutes later, Q posted again.

> Apr 8 2018 00:24:59 (EST)
> Tracking good.
> Relay back channel S-WH-E-P1.
> Fly High.
> Q

The White House was tracking operators, which appear to have been airborne. Messages were relayed on a secure (back) channel between aircraft operating in Syrian (S) airspace and the White House (WH) on an emergency (E) basis. The communications were given top priority (P1). Fly high was probably a wish from Q that the mission would be successful.

Twenty-four minutes later, Q posted again.

> Apr 8 2018 00:48:59
> They are trying to start a war.

> Deflection.
> Public interest shift.
> Pullout announcement.
> Chem attack.
> Coincidence?
> These people are sick.
> Q

The chemical attack in Douma happened on April 7th, the day before this post. The next day (the day of the above post), President Trump announced his intent to withdraw U.S. troops from the region. According to Q, the Syrian president's allies were trying to provoke a war, which is why Q continually stressed that the operational goal was avoiding escalation.

An anon proposed a theory about the motives of Vladimir Putin and Xi Jinping.

> **Anonymous** • Apr 8 2018
> Putin is Russias President.
> His job is to look after the Russian people.
> Put yourself in his shoes.
> He wants to win why not take advantage of his enemies.
> Trump comes along.
> Russia/Putin becomes our Ally
> Xi becomes our Ally
> Xi and Putin are also under attack by the deepstate which is rooted Globally

Q responded.

> Apr 8 2018 11:09:57
> POTUS NEVER telegraphs his moves.
> Think logically.
> Why did POTUS announce his intention to pull out of Syria?
> Moves and countermoves.
> These people are STUPID (& SICK)
> Q

Q pointed out that President Trump never telegraphs his moves. Therefore, since he announced his intent to pull U.S. troops out of the region, he was actually planning an offensive attack, and the announcement was intended to keep his opponents off guard.

On April 13th, Q posted the following message.

> Apr 13 2018
> Trust POTUS.
> Sparrow Red.
> Missiles only.
> Intel good.
> Q

The following day, headlines announced a joint airstrike by French, U.K., and U.S. forces against three Syrian targets. One of the targets was the Barzah scientific research center in Damascus, a facility known to be involved in Syria's chemical weapons program. The Pentagon later announced the facility was hit by 19 JASSM missiles fired from two B1 Lancer bombers. That detail takes us back to this post from April 8th.

> Apr 8 2018
> ♦♦♦
> Auth B19-2.
> Sparrow Red.

The letter-number combination B1 is found in the post, which was the type of bomber used. The number 2 was found in the post, which was the number of bombers. The number 19 was included, which was the number of missiles fired. Is this just a coincidence, or did Q know that two B1 bombers would launch 19 missiles in an airstrike eight days before it happened?

CHAPTER 5

We Don't Say His Name

PRESIDENT TRUMP HELD RALLIES AT various locations around the country during the 2018 election season. From time to time, he would retell the story of when the Senate voted to repeal the Affordable Care Act (also known as Obamacare). President Trump would explain the setup to the vote and then tell how Arizona Senator John McCain disappointed him by unexpectedly voting against the measure at the eleventh hour. Strangely, Trump would never mention McCain by name—a fact that the press found hard to ignore.

A June 24th, 2018, article in *Slate* noted how Donald Trump, while addressing a crowd at a rally, spoke disparagingly about Senator John McCain, who voted against a bill that would have repealed the Affordable Care Act. The article emphasized that President Trump never mentioned McCain's name once.

On August 13th, 2018, *The New York Times* published an article with the following headline: *Trump Talks for 28 Minutes on Bill Named for John McCain. Not Mentioned: McCain.*

Q explained on November 1st, 2017 that people close to President Trump don't like to say McCain's name.

Nov 1 2017
Follow up to last post.
Return to comments re: Pelosi and John M (some of us refuse to say his last name for a reason).

Three days later, on November 4th, 2017, members of the Saudi royal family were arrested. Q asked what donations were made to the nonprofits named after American politicians by Saudi Arabia (SA).

Nov 4 2017
♦♦♦
Martial law declared in SA.
Why is this relevant?
How much money was donated to CF by SA?
How much money was donated to John M Institute by SA?
How much money was donated to Pelosi Foundation?
How much money was donated to CS by SA?
What other bad actors have been paid by SA (bribed)(Not just D's)?
♦♦♦

In this post, Q called into question the nonprofits of Bill Clinton (CF is short for the Clinton Foundation), John McCain, Nancy Pelosi, and Chuck Schumer (CS). Q suggested that foreign governments bribe American politicians by donating money to their nonprofits. Technically, money contributed to a nonprofit can't be used for personal expenses, but later Q hinted that politicians had found a way around the law.

In another post, Q suggested that Chicago-based Loop Capital was involved in transferring money from foreign governments to nonprofits and the politicians they're named after.

Jan 13 2018
LOOP CAPITAL.
CEOs/BODs PAYING TO PLAY.
>Slush Fund
>>Hussein [1] $29,000,000 SINGAPORE
>>We don't say his name [2] $19,000,000 SINGAPORE
(Why don't we say his name?)
>>HRC/BC [3] $15,000,000 Banco de MEXICO

>>NP [4] $8,000,000 Deutsche Bank USA
..........ON......AND.......>ON.......
FOLLOW THE MONEY.
FOCUS on loudest voices in WASH.
Net Worth?
Reconcile?
Q

Q proposed that one way to pay a politician for a political favor is to make them a member of the board of directors or appoint them CEO of a corporation and then give them money in the form of an honorarium. Strictly speaking, such compensation would not appear to be a bribe. Still, if it came from a foreign government, and if the politician took official action favorable to that nation, in effect, it would be a bribe. Q questioned the financial dealings of Barack (Hussein) Obama, John McCain (We don't say his name), Hillary and Bill Clinton, and Nancy Pelosi.

When Q wants to indicate that a particular person is about to leave their place of power, he does so by using their name, the word "fly," and a pair of hashtags. For example, before Representative Al Franken resigned from Congress in December of 2017, Q posted this:

Dec 5 2017
#FLYALFLY#
Runway lights being turned on.
FLY HIGH.
Q

John McCain's middle name was Sidney. In December of 2017, Q confirmed that his tripcode was working on 4chan and suggested that McCain's time in public office was growing short.

Dec 14 2017
Trip code on 4 working.
#FLYSIDFLY#
We don't like to say his name.
Q

In February of 2018, Q posted a message that contained several links and a photo of Senator McCain meeting with leaders of a Syrian militia.

Feb 11 2018
WDSHN_ISIS_TRAITOR_NN.jpg
We don't say his name returning to prime time.
Wonder if his so-called illness/condition will flare up.
"He's not a war hero."
He's a mega millionaire.
M-Institute.
https://www.mccaininstitute.org/donors/
Rothschild/Clintons/SA/etc.
[Not complete].
https://www.washingtonpost.com/news/fact-checker/wp/2016/04/08/john-mccains-claim-he-has-nothing-to-do-with-the-mccain-institute/?utm_term=.0e635aaf76b1
https://www.zerohedge.com/news/2017-03-08/mccain-institutes-failure-use-donations-anti-trafficking-purposes-raises-questions
Define money laundering.
Define the word 'Traitor'.
A world w/o this man is a world better off.
Q

One of the links in the post was to an article by *Disobedient Media*. The article explained that although the McCain Institute claims to focus on battling human trafficking, a review of their IRS filings showed they were not spending money on that cause. In 2012, the Institute received $8,685,619 in donations, gifts, and grants. Their expenses that year amounted to $500,000, and the same amount was spent in 2013, though none of it was used to combat human trafficking.

The photograph included in the above post became the subject of much debate. It was first released as part of an announcement on May 27th, 2013, that McCain had secretly traveled to Syria to meet with leaders of the Free Syrian Army. The photo showed McCain meeting with a group of men, one of whom was identified as Brigadier General Idriss Salem, the head of the Free Syrian Army. A second person was identified as Abu Bakr al-Baghdadi, the founder of ISIS, who was listed among the top five most wanted terrorists by the U.S. government.

The left-leaning website *PolitiFact* claimed the man in the photo was not al-Baghdadi, but someone who looked like him. However, they refused to disclose the name of the supposed look-alike, citing concerns for his safety. Q sometimes provides more information about a photo through the filename of the image. Part of the filename for the photo attached to this post is "ISIS_TRAITOR."

On April 4th, 2018, Q gave anons the news that the Arizona Senator would not be seeking re-election.

> Apr 4 2018
> We don't say his name.
> Adios.
> The protected flow into AZ is no more.
> Under the cover of his health, he will not be seeking another term.
> Q

There was a hint in this post that Senator McCain of Arizona shielded illegal activities across the Arizona-Mexico border. Q elaborated on that topic in another post the same day.

> Apr 4 2018
> Troops to Border.
> Clown Black Ops.
> Private funds.
> Raised how?
> Troops @ Border does what?
> Impact?
> To who?
> D's involved.
> MS_13/Illegals road block.
> Sex traffic road block.
> Children road block.
> Drugs road block.
> Guns road block.
> China/Russia pass-through-intel-pull road block.
> Name we don't say AZ road block.
> Jeff Flake AZ road block.
> Big money TERMINATE.
> The WALL means more than you know.
> The FIGHT for the WALL is for so much more.
> Q

Q implied that certain politicians in Arizona facilitated the flow of human trafficking, weapons trafficking, and drug trafficking through the southern U.S. border. The phrase, Clown Black Ops, seems to suggest that some of these operations were conducted covertly by the CIA. When President Trump declared a national emergency and sent troops to the southern border, they acted as a roadblock to these activities. The wall on the southern border would permanently end the majority of illegal trafficking if it could be completed.

Four days later, Q asked about the real purpose of McCain's secret meeting in Syria and suggested there would be reports about his declining health, which would provide a cover for the consequences of his past transgressions.

> Apr 8 2018
> No name in Syria.
> Timeline.
> Purpose?
> Who attended?
> No name panic.
> Health cover.
> Fast.
> Q

About an hour later, Q posted a photo taken during a trip by Senator McCain to Syria. He asked anons to find the location where the photo was taken. Appearing in the picture were McCain and several Syrian nationals, including Abu Bakr al-Baghdadi. The building in the background had spiderwebs drawn on the windows.

> Apr 8 2018 16:33:03
> Location.
> Exact location.
> Q

Six minutes later, Q asked what contractors shadowed McCain.

> Apr 8 2018 16:39:06
> Pictures leaked for this very moment.
> Who/what is not pictured?

What forces shadowed No Name?
Contractors.
Special contractors.
What was delivered?
Smiles.
Exact location.
Exact.
Buildings E of spider web.
Spider web marker.
Open source.
Q

Eight minutes later, Q posted once more. Included in this post was a link to an article about Erik Prince, the founder of the private contracting firm Blackwater.

Apr 8 2018 16:47:12
https://www.politico.com/blogs/laurarozen/1209/Report_Blackwater_CEO_Eric_Prince_was_CIA_asset.html
Think Double.
Why are we confirming this publicly?
Why now?
Q

The linked article explained that Erik Prince served with the CIA. Was Q hinting that he acted as a double agent? The implication was that Prince gathered information about bad actors in the CIA and gave it to patriots. This appears to suggest that the contractors Q mentioned in the previous post were with Blackwater.

Apr 8 2018
Why did HUSSEIN PROTECT ISIS?
POTUS ISIS focus and destroy 1 year?
vs HUSSEIN 8 years?
vs GWB?
DC access.
Sold out.
Bring back the gallows!
Q

Q pointed out that President Trump destroyed the caliphate of ISIS in a little more than a year while Barack Obama had eight years in office and made no progress. Did Obama covertly provide aid to them?

On April 21st, 2018, Q posted an article about Huma Abedin's ties to the terror organization Muslim Brotherhood.

> Apr 21 2018 23:28:19 (EST)
> http://thehill.com/blogs/pundits-blog/presidential-campaign/292310-huma-abedins-ties-to-the-muslim-brotherhood
> Good article.
> Don't forget about Huma.
> AWAN.
> VJ.
> ………
> FBI.
> America for sale.
> Betrayal.
> Treason.
> No name.
> Inside out destruction.
> SA.
> SA.
> SA.
> HUMA & Hussein.
> http://harvardmuslimalumni.org/about
> Who paid?
> SA [vital].
> Q

Huma Abedin was Hillary Clinton's personal assistant. Q implicated her, Barack Obama's assistant Valerie Jarrett (VJ), and Senator McCain as traitors who sold out America to foreign nations like Saudi Arabia (SA).

On April 30th, 2018, the day Benjamin Netanyahu revealed evidence of Iran's covert nuclear weapons program, Q posted the following message.

> Apr 30 2018
> Define the terms of the Iran nuclear deal.
> Does the agreement define & confine cease & desist 'PRO' to

the republic of Iran?
What if Iran created a classified 'satellite' Nuclear facility in Northern Syria?
What if the program never ceased?
What other bad actors are possibly involved?
Did the U.S. know?
Where did the cash payments go?
How many planes delivered?
Did all planes land in same location?
Where did the U1 material end up?
Is this material traceable?
Yes.
Define cover.
What if U1 material ended up in Syria?
What would be the primary purpose?
SUM OF ALL FEARS.
In the movie, where did the material come from?
What country?
What would happen if Russia or another foreign state supplied Uranium to Iran/Syria?
WAR.
What does U1 provide?
Define cover.
Why did we strike Syria?
Why did we really strike Syria?
Define cover.
Patriots in control.
Q

According to Q, the Iran nuclear deal was favorable to Iran, which is why its details were kept from Congress and the public. The agreement removed Iran's sanctions, allowing them to obtain the supplies necessary to continue their nuclear weapons program. News reports confirm that there was a secret nuclear facility in Northern Syria.

Q asked questions about *The Sum of All Fears*, a novel by Tom Clancy, where a sociopath tried to trick the U.S. and Russia into starting a nuclear war. In the film, the plan was to get the two superpowers to destroy one another and then set up a fascist superstate, headquartered in Europe.

Some world leaders believe that war results from the existence of independent nation-states. They claim nations must wage war to exert their national sovereignty. The solution they propose is to have all independent nation-states surrender their sovereignty to a global government. Two countries have caused problems for those who pursue this goal—the United States and Russia, which have refused to surrender their sovereignty.

One way to establish a global government would be to start a limited nuclear war. The devastation caused by such a war would become the justification for the eradication of borders. Q has suggested that rogue nations like Iran and North Korea were permitted (under the watchful eye of the CIA) to develop nuclear weapons to start a war with Russia or the United States. Either scenario would move the world one step closer to their goal.

The sale of the North American company Uranium One to the Russian company Rosatom enriched the Clinton Foundation, but it also allowed Russia to obtain a large amount of uranium from the U.S. and Canada. Q implied that some of the uranium was secretly diverted to Syria, where it was used to build weapons of mass destruction.

As Q mentioned, batches of uranium have unique radiologic fingerprints, and they can be traced. If anyone caught on that Iran had obtained uranium, it would be traced back to the batch sold to Russia, and Russia would be blamed for it. Q suggested that the U.S. airstrikes on the Syrian airbase on April 7th, 2017, were not (primarily) for the reason that was publicly given. Instead, the strikes were a cover to allow patriots in the military to obtain the evidence they needed to expose the illegal scheme.

In his post from April 8th, 2018, Q asked what was delivered when John McCain visited Syria. The sale of Uranium One to the Russian energy company Rosatom was a complicated deal that took years to finalize, but the transfer was complete by January of 2013. McCain's trip to Syria was in May of 2013. Did Q suggest that the Senator oversaw a shipment of uranium to Syria and that contractors from Blackwater were surveilling him?

On May 10th, 2018, President Trump posted the following tweet.

Donald J. Trump (from his Twitter account):
Five Most Wanted leaders of ISIS just captured!
7:33 AM - 10 May 2018

Q responded, suggesting that Senator McCain's previous meetings with the leaders of ISIS were about to be revealed and that "No Name" would be contemplating his exit strategy.

> May 10 2018 10:15:01 (EST)
> https://mobile.twitter.com/realDonaldTrump/status/994586105822564353
> Names?
> No Name prev meeting(s)?
> Panic?
> Discussions of death/funeral?
> Medical or escape?
> Now comes the pain.
> Q

Q has an odd way of predicting the timing of future events. General Mike Flynn was referred for prosecution as part of Robert Mueller's investigation of alleged Russian interference in the 2016 Presidential election. The former three-star general pleaded guilty to one count of making materially false statements and cooperated with the investigation. It was later discovered that senior officials at James Comey's FBI acted in a way that set Flynn up for a fall.

In March of 2018, an anon asked Q to make sure that Flynn would be free from the bogus charges.

> **Anonymous** • Mar 27 2018
> Free Flynn

Q replied.

> Done in 30.
> House cleaning.
> WH secured.
> Final stage.
> Q

Exactly one month later, on April 27th, 2018, the House Intelligence Committee released the results of its investigation into Russian election interference. Their report cleared General Flynn of any wrongdoing.

Q responded to the news.

> Apr 27 2018
> "Done in 30."
> [30]
> http://www.foxnews.com/politics/2018/04/27/house-report-backs-claim-that-fbi-agents-did-not-think-flynn-lied-despite-guilty-plea.html
> Why would Flynn plead guilty to something untrue?
> Define testimony.
> Define 'on record'.
> Who knows where the bodies are buried?
> Flynn is safe.
> Expand your thinking.
> Q

In June 2018, Q asked about the conspicuous absence of the then-senator from Arizona he calls "no name."

> Jun 18 2018
> No name absent.
> End near?
> Q

In one of the most prescient posts ever dropped by Q, on July 25th, 2018, he posted a picture of Senator McCain and said he would be returning to the headlines. In the photo, McCain's eyes were closed, and his hands were held up with his palms facing toward the camera. The timestamp of the post was 16:28 mountain time (4:28 pm).

> Jul 25 2018 16:28:35 (MST)
> 6169C31C-A4BA-4CCD-8561-D900C8C16307.jpeg
> No name returning to headlines.
> Q

One month later, on August 25th, it was announced that Senator McCain had died. *The New York Times* reported, "Mr. McCain died at 4:28 p.m. local time." The Senator died exactly one month to the minute after Q said he would be returning to the headlines.

Aug 26 2018
Suicide weekend?
Hands up?
[30]
[0:28]
Impossible?
Coincidence?
We are in control.
BIG week ahead.
Q

CHAPTER 6

This is Not a Game

SOME PEOPLE CONSIDER Q'S OPERATION to be a game of words, but a close inspection of the posts shows otherwise. Q provides periodic reports on clandestine military operations going on around the globe. Although detailed reports cannot be provided for reasons of operational security, the information given suggests that some activities involve life and death situations.

> Nov 5 2017
> Please pray.
> Operators are in harms way.
> High risk.
> High value targets.
> Please pause and give thanks to those who would die to save our republic.
> More to follow.
> Q

Q's mission itself is not a game, but the way in which information is disseminated is something like a game of 20 questions.

One day, an anon asked Q to confirm that bad actors would face justice.

> **Anonymous** • Mar 8 2018
> Q, please tell us it's still NO DEALS!
> And that this people will face JUSTICE!! Please just say YES.
> They will. I pray so hard every night!

Q replied.

> NO DEALS!
> We work for you.
> We listen to you.
> You pushed the IBOR and immediately POTUS began to comment/take action re: social media.
> PLAY THE GAME WITH US.
> Q

Q affirmed that criminals in high places would not be offered deals. As a show of support, when anons pushed for an internet bill of rights (IBOR) President Trump pressured Congress to change the laws that regulate internet privacy and censorship. The anon responded.

> **Anonymous** • Mar 8 2018
> BEST GAME EVER BOSS!!!
> > TV Time!!!

Q replied.

> Mar 8 2018
> Everything has meaning.
> This is not a game.
> Learn to play the game.
> Q

The disciples of Jesus asked why he taught in parables. He said it was to reveal the truth to those who had ears to hear while concealing it from those with darkened hearts. Q posts riddles for the same reason. There are many people following his posts. Some are friends. Others are enemies. The enemies are mostly rogue operatives from foreign and domestic intelligence agencies who are working against President Trump. Q needs to convey factual information to the researchers working with him and the President while providing disinformation to enemies.

> Nov 11 2017
> Rogue operators are here.
> Failed to shut down site.
> Protected.
> This will only get worse.
> Archive and coordinate.
> Crumbs dropped will soon paint the full picture.
> The picture will open the eyes of the world.
> We can't do it without you.
> God bless you all.
> Q

Although rogue agents continually try to shut down the website on which Q posts, his messages still get out.

In November of 2017, Q was training anons to put together his clues to paint the picture of events that were happening on the global stage. The lesson was not going well. An anon expressed his frustration.

> **Anonymous** • Nov 21 2017
> Dear Q:
> Jesus Christ was fu****g pissed at his apostles most of the time because they were stupid f***s (at the time) that couldn't piece together even the most basic of clues. We are no different and are even more clueless. We are trying, but you really do have to spell it out for us. Sorry. We believe you are speaking the truth. To whom else can we turn? So put up with our shit and help us, and we'll do what you ask.

Q's reply came later.

> Feb 11 2018
> Sniffer progs would kill the site.
> Everything has to be carefully crafted and tooled prior to release.
> Godspeed, Patriot.

By using codes, anagrams, symbols, riddles, and double meanings, Q creates a degree of uncertainty that keeps everyone guessing. While it's frustrating to be uncertain about the meaning of some posts, the ambiguity is necessary. Q's messages are carefully prepared so as not to give away vital information to enemies, who use sophisticated artificial intelligence programs (sniffer progs) to interpret them. Although uncertainty is baked into the dough that makes up Q's posts, when news stories drop, we can look back and find a trail of crumbs showing Q's foreknowledge. But Q's goal isn't merely to prove that he's an intelligence insider. His foreknowledge gives anons confidence that their research is not done in vain.

Some people intentionally make false claims and predictions based on Q's posts. When their predictions don't come true, they use them to discredit Q. For example, in June of 2018, a Twitter account called Eye the Spy predicted that Julian Assange (JA) would be freed by June 11th. His predictions were supposedly based on Q's posts. The user then posted on the research board, feigning disappointment and claiming that Q was a phony (a LARP).

> **Anonymous** • Jun 11 2018
> 6/11 ALMOST OVER
> NO BOOMS, NO JA, NO ARRESTS
> YES LARP

Q responded.

> When did we mention/emphasize the 11th?
> Those with an agenda to discredit are pushing false information.
> They (you) will fail.
> Learn.
> Use logic.
> Q

Q might be able to determine someone's allegiance and motives by the content of a post, or he may be able to identify troublemakers by their IP address. Q generally doesn't respond to enemies or confirm their decodes except when he wants to expose them or send them down the wrong trail.

One criticism of Q is that his posts are written in such a way that when a significant event happens, he could then falsely claim to have predicted it by decoding a previous message in a way that supports his claim. This concern speaks to Q's integrity. I've come to trust Q because he has, at times, refused to claim credit for an interesting event when he could have said he planned it that way. During his mission, Q has posted at exactly the same time President Trump tweeted on more than 30 occasions, usually preceding the President by a few seconds. When Q and the President post simultaneously, it creates what Q calls a "zero delta."

In the following post, an anon noted that Q and President Trump posted at the same time.

> **Anonymous** • Dec 12 2018
> ClipboardImage.png
> 0 delta
> Q/POTUS

Q responded, saying the timing of their posts was not intentional, but a coincidence.

> Not intended.
> Separated by 2.
> Q

Another concern is that Q's messages are so ambiguous that five people may interpret the same post in five different ways. This is a valid observation. I've seen many people claim to have correctly decoded a post that no one else had figured out or claim that others had decoded a message incorrectly. This approach ignores the fact that Q regularly confirms correct decodes. Q interacts with researchers and encourages the exploration of particular topics while providing additional information and confirmation to those who are doing accurate work.

Initially, the only way to have your work confirmed was to post it on 4chan (later 8chan and then 8kun) and hope that Q responded to you. More recently, Q monitored other platforms. For example, I've posted a decode on Twitter only to see it appear on the research board ten minutes later with more information or a question from Q. When I see one of my theories confirmed or when Q asks a clarifying question about my post, I take the theory one step further or do more research on the subject. If the next guess is correct, Q will confirm it. There is no need to argue over whether a decode is valid. If it has not been confirmed by Q, it remains just a theory.

An anon summarized Q's operation this way:

> **Anonymous** • Apr 9 2018
> Keep in mind that every crumb is not meant to be solved before the event. Some of the drops are things for anons to dig on and make connections with, others are markers for future reference.
> >[future proves past]
> Some drops are just simply communication to the anons. What needs to be understood to appreciate whats going here is the fact the Q is basically creating a circular flow diagram that can be referenced and cross-checked with news releases. Q can't just disclose specifics about a situation or operation without violating security protocol. Instead they drop questions and statements that lead to answers that can be understood once the subject becomes public. This provides the validation necessary for the public to believe The Great Awakening is legit. Disinformation and misdirection with Q is real. In other words Q is pointing over there but really the focus is here and only until you publicly get the news can you go back and understand. (Think SA drops) All of this is accomplished without giving up specific details about the operation. It's quite genius.

CHAPTER 7

The Anatomy of a Smear Campaign

COUNTLESS ARTICLES CONTINUED TO BE published by the mainstream media attacking Q and his followers. In this chapter, we'll examine the tactics used by the press in developing these articles and the motives behind them.

Citizen Journalists

In November of 2016, while speaking at a public event, General Michael Flynn noted that corporate journalists had abdicated their responsibilities. Rather than fairly and objectively reporting the news, they had become political activists. Average citizens saw this as an opportunity, and began publishing their own news on social media.

Historically, the flow of information has been controlled through centralized news networks because expensive equipment was needed to air broadcasts and print newspapers. Today, anyone can be a print journalist by setting up their own website. Most citizen journalists establish influential platforms on social media sites. A mobile phone can function as a broadcast studio, and thousands of ordinary people now create their own news shows.

Having exclusive access to sources of information, career journalists have enjoyed an advantage over the public. But Q has changed that dynamic. Q is a source of information similar to those used by journalists. His messages help ordinary people understand current events. Unlike the media, Q does not provide an information narrative. His posts consist of raw information. Some messages require research before they can be understood. Readers can interpret the posts however they choose. Some bits of information must be synthesized together with others and then contextualized. The view of current events developed by those who follow Q differs from that of the mainstream media.

The media understand the threat citizen journalists pose to their control of information. Ordinary people now occupy the roles they once filled. To counter this threat, the corporate press developed a plan to discredit the source of information used by some citizen journalists. The plan centered around a smear campaign against Q. Elements of the campaign can be found in an August 8, 2018 *Bloomberg* article titled, *QAnon Is Running Amok, and the Time Has Come for Interventions.* (The article is no longer available on Bloomberg's website, but is available on the Internet Archive Wayback Machine.)

Let's look at a quote from the article:

> *Memes emanating from the conspiracy group—which are tenuously united in the discredited belief that there's a plot to oust Trump from the presidency—have made their way into the social media accounts of everyone from Michael Flynn (who was briefly national security adviser) to White House social media adviser Dan Scavino. Sometimes these memes can be as innocent as an image featuring Trump with a QAnon slogan (as was the case for Scavino), but at other times they take on more sinister overtones such as the oath to QAnon—"Where we go one, we go all"—which Flynn posted on July 4.*

Bloomberg attempted to smear the reputation of General Flynn, who seemed supportive of the Q movement at the time. Flynn had followed many anons on social media and interacted with them through private messages. His family took the same oath taken by thousands of Q followers, as shown in a video he posted on his Twitter account on July 4th. *Bloomberg* falsely reported that the oath taken by some Q followers was to Q, when it was taken *to the United States*. Flynn's oath (the same one taken by anyone who joins the military) was called "sinister." One goal of the media's smear campaign is convincing the public that Q followers have nefarious motives for their actions.

The media know that Q intends to expose corruption. That exposure includes piecing together evidence in the public domain regarding the Obama administration's attempt to prevent Donald Trump from being elected and then trying to remove him from office. Those attempts included the FBI's Crossfire Hurricane investigation, the Mueller investigation, and impeachment. In the above quote, *Bloomberg* referred to this plot as a "discredited belief," despite the fact that several U.S. Attorneys are currently investigating this crime, and one—John Durham—recently indicted a co-conspirator, Michael Sussman. A second goal of the press is convincing the public that every idea proposed by Q followers is a baseless conspiracy.

Anything but the Actual Posts

Mainstream articles rarely discuss Q's posts because that would cause people to read them. Instead, the media have developed a cluster of topics they know the public will find either ridiculous or repulsive. For example, the *Bloomberg* article asserted that Q followers are obsessed with conspiracies, like the idea that Tom Hanks has a sex slave, as this quote from the article illustrates:

> *Everyone else in the family remembers the stir that corner caused when they claimed that Tom Hanks had a sex slave.*

In any cross-section of the population, you're likely to find a few people who believe Tom Hanks has a sex slave. In the truther community, that belief is more common. However, Q has never mentioned Tom Hanks in any of his posts. To discredit the movement, the media claim that Q is obsessed with subjects he has never mentioned.

Like thousands of articles before it, the *Bloomberg* story lampooned a post they attributed to Q without providing the post itself or the context necessary to understand it. The article referenced what is commonly believed to be Q's first post. Nearly everyone who has read this post (including experienced researchers) believes this message was posted by Q, but it was not. The post in question (shown below) includes both the original post number from the 4chan board and the user ID number.

Anonymous • ID: gb953qGI No.147005381
Oct 28 2017 14:33:50
Hillary Clinton will be arrested between 7:45 AM - 8:30 AM EST on Monday - the morning on Oct 30, 2017.

Note the user ID number of the above post: **gb953qGI**. Each time a user posts, the board automatically assigns an anonymous user ID to their IP address. That user ID appears on all posts during a session. The user ID of this post is not the user ID assigned to Q that day. The post below was Q's response to this post.

ID: BQ7V3bcW No.147012719
Oct 28 2017 15:44:28 (EST)
>>147005381
HRC extradition already in motion effective yesterday with several countries in case of cross border run. Passport approved to be flagged effective 10/30 @ 12:01am. Expect massive riots organized in defiance and others fleeing the US to occur. US M's will conduct the operation while NG activated. Proof check: Locate a NG member and ask if activated for duty 10/30 across most major cities.

Note the user ID of the above post: **BQ7V3bcW**. This ID number is different from the one on the original post and it is same as the one on a post by Q an hour and a half later.

ID: BQ7V3bcW No.147023341
Oct 28 2017 17:15:48 (EST)
Mockingbird
HRC detained, not arrested (yet).
♦♦♦

Q responded to the original post saying Hillary (HRC) had been detained but not arrested. To understand the purpose of this post and others like it, you must follow a string of related messages from that same week and put them together.

Three days after the above post, on October 31st, 2017, Q predicted that the indictments of John Podesta and Huma Abedin would happen on November 3rd and November 6th, respectively:

The Anatomy of a Smear Campaign

> Oct 31 2017
> There are more good people than bad. The wizards and warlocks (inside term) will not allow another Satanic Evil POS control our country. Realize Soros, Clintons, Obama, Putin, etc. are all controlled by 3 families (the 4th was removed post Trump's victory).
> 11.3 - Podesta indicted
> 11.6 - Huma indicted
> Manafort was placed into Trump's camp (as well as others). The corruption that will come out is so serious that deals must be cut for people to walk away otherwise 70% of elected politicians would be in jail (you are seeing it already begin). A deep cleaning is occurring and the prevention and defense of pure evil is occurring on a daily basis. They never thought they were going to lose control of the Presidency (not just D's) and thought they had control since making past mistakes (JFK, Reagan).
> Good speed, Patriots.
> PS, Soros is targeted.

Many have pointed out that this prediction did not come to pass. Before we assume this was just another failed prediction, let's read on. The next day, November 1st, Q said proofs would begin on November 3rd.

> Nov 1 2017
> Follow up to last post.
> Return to comments re: Pelosi and John M (some of us refuse to say his last name for a reason).
> This all has meaning - everything stated. Big picture stuff - few positions allow for this direct knowledge.
> Proof to begin 11.3.
> We all sincerely appreciate the work you do. Keep up the good fight. The flow of information is vital.
> God bless.

Saudi Arabia

Publicly available records show that the Saudi royal family donated between 10 million and 25 million dollars to the Clinton Foundation. It's natural to wonder if they expected political favors in return for their generosity. Some have suggested that the Clintons were little more than the political assets of the Saudis.

Imagine you're a member of the Saudi royal family, and you learn that an anonymous person claiming to be an intelligence insider is predicting the imminent arrest and indictment of your most valuable assets. (At the time, Huma Abedin was Hillary Clinton's assistant. John Podesta was her 2016 campaign manager.) Would you take action to try to prevent their arrest the first week of November?

Imagine your surprise when you or your royal family members are arrested on the morning of November 4th, instead of Clinton, Podesta, and Abedin.

On November 4th, 2017, the day of the arrest of members of the Saudi royal family, an anon realized that in addition to hints about Hillary Clinton, Podesta, and Abedin, Q had also been dropping hints about events in Saudi Arabia.

Anonymous • Nov 4 2017
WAIT
WAIT
WAIT
GO BACK TO THE POST ABOUT THE FAMILES THAT RUN EVERYTHING AND TRUMP TAKING ONE OUT
WAS ONE OF THEM THIS SAUDI FAMILY
SERIOUSLY
BECAUSE THAT MAKES THIS A HAPPENING
I Remember the phrasing not making sense, I was like "oh does he mean that dt took out the Clintons?" But the Clintons were on the list as remaining so I didn't know who was taken out

Q responded.

Nov 4 2017
Very smart, Anon.
Disinformation is real.
Distractions are necessary.
SA is the primary, US is secondary, (Asia/EU)...
Alice & Wonderland.
Q

Q explained that the arrest of corrupt political figures would begin in Saudi Arabia and move to the U.S. and other countries. The threat that American political figures would be arrested was a diversion intended to keep attention on them, while an operation was being planned to arrest their Saudi handlers.

Silence and Violence

The media intend to silence Q and his followers. Several tactics have been employed to achieve that objective. Early on, the press claimed that because Q chose to post on 4chan, he must be aligned with white supremacists who also post there. That's like saying if you post videos on YouTube, you must be sympathetic to terrorists who also post there. The websites 4chan, 8chan, and 8kun have hundreds of message boards. Each board is dedicated to the discussion of a different topic. As is true of Twitter, Facebook, or any other platform, white supremacists are a small cross-section of the user base.

The accusation that Q is connected to white supremacy isn't true. Q has never posted a message espousing racist ideology. If he had, you can be sure the press would have a screenshot of it, and it would be prominently displayed in their articles. Although the claim that Q is connected to white supremacy isn't true, it was a useful tactic by the media.

The media have also tried to tie Q to some form of violent extremism. Because there are no actual ties between Q and acts of violence, the press had to manufacture them. Read a few articles about Q, and you'll notice how reporters go out of their way to make some connection—no matter how far-fetched it might be—between Q and acts of violence. The *Bloomberg* article insinuated, without evidence, that a mass murderer in Germany espoused "'Qanon-like beliefs."

In February, in Hanau, Germany, a lone gunman espousing QAnon-like beliefs massacred nine people in bars frequented by immigrants before killing his mother and himself.

The media have no evidence that Q followers are violent. Such evidence doesn't exist, so indirect evidence must be created. In 2019, *Yahoo News* published an article claiming that the FBI issued a bulletin warning about the threat of violent extremism related to "fringe conspiracy theories" like Qanon. The article centers around a bulletin supposedly published by the FBI's Phoenix Field Office. I decided to investigate the origins of the alleged FBI bulletin.

I contacted Jana Winter, the author of the article, and Michael Isikoff, who was credited with developing the lede for the story. (This is the same Michael Isikoff who publicized the infamous Steele dossier that was used to obtain a FISA warrant to surveil Trump campaign staffer Carter Page.) The document embedded in the *Yahoo News* article was hosted on a private Scribd account. I asked Isikoff and Winter to provide a link to a government website where the FBI bulletin could be found or other information that would validate it. Neither Winter nor Isikoff responded to my request. One would hope they didn't just find the document on Scribd and assume it was legitimate. If they received it from a government source, why not provide information about how they had obtained it?

I contacted the FBI's Phoenix field office. The agent said he could not verify the existence of the bulletin. He suggested I file a FOIA request, and referred me to the Bureau's National Press Office. I searched the FOIA database with no results and filed a new FOIA request with the title of the document as the search query. The FOIA request returned no results.

I contacted the FBI's National Press Office, and they could not confirm the existence of the bulletin. However, they provided links to congressional testimonies of FBI and DOJ officials who addressed this matter, and a link to an FBI article describing the categories they use to define violent extremism. According to an FBI public statement referenced by the National Press Office, the bureau currently has only four categories of domestic violent extremism:

> *The FBI classifies domestic terrorism threats into four main categories: racially motivated violent extremism, anti-government/anti-authority extremism, animal rights/environmental extremism, and abortion extremism.*

https://www.fbi.gov/news/testimony/confronting-the-rise-of-domestic-terrorism-in-the-homeland

One of the links provided by the Press Office pointed to a hearing where FBI Director Christopher Wray testified about violent extremism. Wray said the FBI doesn't "investigate ideology, no matter how repugnant."

When I did a forensic examination of the alleged FBI bulletin, I found a number of artifacts that called its validity into question. I will provide some observations to illustrate my main concerns.

I compared the suspicious FBI bulletin embedded in the *Yahoo News* article to a known FBI bulletin on "Black Identity Violent Extremism," found on the FBI's website. (Note: Black Identity Violent Extremism is no longer a recognized category. It was replaced with the broader category "Racially Motivated Violent Extremism.") The website contains a scanned image (PDF) of the bulletin. Several scanning irregularities were found on it. The *exact same* scanning errors appear in the document featured in the *Yahoo News* article.

Most FBI bulletins contain a customer satisfaction survey. Section one of the survey asks users to evaluate the bulletin's usefulness, and bubbles are provided for responses. Section two asks how the customer plans to use the bulletin in support of their mission. That section has eight possible responses, with a check box to the left of each answer. In this section, the vertical column of check boxes obscured the first few letters of each line of text for the response. The customer satisfaction survey has six sections. The numbers for sections one through three line up in a perfect vertical line, but the numbers for sections four through six are left of the vertical line. All of these oddities in the Black Identity Extremism bulletin appear to be the result of scanning errors.

The *Yahoo News* bulletin on conspiracy extremism has the exact same scanner errors in its customer satisfaction survey.

The bulletin on black identity extremism had a watermark showing the fiscal year 2017. The *Yahoo News* bulletin showed the fiscal year 2019. Despite being issued by different field offices in different years, the same revision date appears at the bottom of both forms on the customer satisfaction survey.

On the last page of the black identity violent extremism bulletin, there is a product serial number that provides a unique tracking number. The product serial number was redacted from the bulletin that appeared in the *Yahoo News* article, making it virtually impossible to track. That step would be necessary if you hoped to pass off a forged document as real.

It's difficult to confidently state that *Yahoo's* bulletin is legitimate, given the FBI's position that they do not investigate ideologies, their official categories of violent extremism, and *Yahoo's* refusal to provide corroborating evidence in light of suspicious findings. Nevertheless, once the bulletin was published, the mainstream articles that followed insisted that the FBI had declared Q a domestic terror threat.

This operation is not unlike the way the FBI obtained a FISA warrant to surveil Carter Page. The information required for surveillance was not readily available, so it was manufactured by Christopher Steele. In its raw form, Steele's information was not admissible as evidence in court, so it was promoted by Michael Isikoff and *Yahoo*. Once it was featured in a recognized news outlet, it was considered to be validated, and it became admissible as evidence. Thus, the surveillance of Carter Page became the pretext to smear the Trump Presidential campaign and, later, the pretext for the Mueller investigation. Did Isikoff and *Yahoo* contrive the FBI bulletin for the same purpose—to give it credibility and use it to smear their enemy?

The Streisand Effect

In 2003, a photographer published a photo of Barbara Streisand's home in Malibu, California. Streisand sued the photographer and tried to have the photo removed from the internet. Her efforts only created greater public interest in seeing her home.

Thanks to efforts by the media, the Q movement is growing faster than ever. A 2020 internal audit by Facebook uncovered thousands of Q groups and pages with millions of members. What did they expect would happen after publishing more than 3,000 articles slamming the so-called irrelevant, fringe, kooky, unhinged, dangerous internet conspiracy known as Q? The rapid growth of the movement was the thrust of *Bloomberg's* article. When they weren't comparing Q to ISIS, they were whining about how the movement is becoming normalized.

> *The conspiracy isn't going to go away soon and, as the Republican Party begins to count on QAnoners for votes, its paranoid style is almost on the verge of political normalization.*

> *In one important aspect, though, QAnon is like Islamic State: Adherents often start from a feeling of alienation and then acquire an unquestioning faith in the righteousness of a cause that gives vent to their frustrations.*

The Endgame

After convincing the public that Q is a violent movement, the next step was convincing tech companies. Social media and internet providers were pressured to de-platform anyone giving a voice to Q. (After all, they wouldn't want to support terrorists, would they?)

Since December of 2017, Q had been posting on 8chan. Insinuations that 8chan supported violence led to tech providers cutting off their services. That silenced Q during the three months it took 8chan's owner, Jim Watkins, to set up another website—8kun.

On January 6th, 2021, thousands of patriots showed up to hear President Trump and others speak in Washington D.C. near the Capitol. The media and members of Congress have since weaponized the incident claiming that supporters of Q tried to overthrow the government.

Two days later, on January 8th, 2021, Twitter suspended the accounts of patriots and Q followers, justifying the move by claiming that the suspended account owners engaged in "offline harm" (violence).

However, in 2023, video evidence came to light that contradicts the reporting of the media. Jacob Chansley, the so-called "Qanon shaman" was portrayed by the press as a mentally unstable and violent person-ideo recordings obtained by Fox News showed Chansley calmly strolling through the halls of the Capitol building being escorted by police. One video showed Chansley speaking into a megaphone telling the crowd to disperse after President Trump asked protesters to leave.

The media insist that the January 6th protest was organic, but videos show Ray Epps, a known federal informant, trying to spur protesters to enter the Capitol building. FBI whistleblowers have testified before Congress that at least 100 federal agents or informants were embedded in the crowd on January 6th. The DOJ admitted in a legal filing that 40 informants were present among the Proud Boys that day.

This information paints a different picture from the narrative created by the media about the January 6th protest. But the damage was already done. Once society believes a group is violent, the group can be attacked financially. PayPal, Patreon, Payoneer, PopMoney, Venmo, and other payment processors closed my personal and business accounts without warning. They suspended the accounts of many other law-abiding patriots who report on Q. This wasn't just the icing on the cake for the media; it was mission accomplished. Making it nearly impossible for Q researchers to earn a living seems to have been their objective all along.

CHAPTER 8

Taking the Red Pill

IN A POPULAR FILM TITLED *The Matrix*, humans are enslaved in a virtual world created by artificial intelligence. What they perceive to be reality is a computer simulation. They're kept in a state of subdued compliance, living out their lives in a digital simulation, not knowing that what seems to be real is merely the manifestation of computer code.

Art imitates life. The lives we currently live are not all that different from the way they are portrayed in *The Matrix*. Part of Q's mission is gradually awakening us to the shocking reality of our true state of existence.

>Nov 5 2017
>♦♦♦
>The complete picture would put 99% of Americans (the World) in a hospital.
>♦♦♦

The beginning of my awakening happened as it often does through a dream from God. In the dream, I sat beside a man who said my understanding of history was false. He explained how various events from the past really transpired. He asked many questions. "How are these people and events

The Q Chronicles • Book 3: This Is Not a Game

connected? Why is this relevant?" He reminded me of Q and impressed upon me the idea that I should take his words seriously.

Because I tend to accept official explanations of historical events, I've never had much curiosity about alternative explanations and narratives. Yet, in the dream, God delivered a message to me through the inquisitive man that I had accepted false explanations and narratives.

Identity, etiquette, opinions, religions, laws, economics, and government are mental constructs that exist inside our minds. If I asked you to point to a cat, you could do so without using words, but if I asked you to point to the government, you would need to create a mental picture using words.

A narrative of society has been programmed into our minds through exposure to movies, podcasts, TV news, books, classes, and political speeches. I didn't know the narrative I accepted was false. Like someone trapped inside the matrix, I became a compliant servant of a sinister system—the framework of which I could not see, and the details of which I was ignorant.

The main character of *The Matrix*, Neo, knows something isn't right. He can't quite put his finger on it, but he knows things are not as they appear. Because he's never been outside the matrix, he has no concept of reality or the true nature of his existence. Someone who has been outside offers him a chance to see the world as it really is.

The high point of the film is the offer to Neo to take one of two pills. If he chooses to take a blue pill, he remains inside the matrix with his current belief system intact. The narrative of the world he's been given may be false, but he's familiar with it, which offers some comfort. The other option is taking a red pill and having all his beliefs destroyed and replaced with a completely unknown but accurate view of the world.

Mar 28 2018
MSM talking about red v. blue pill?
Matrix reference?
Coincidence?
Q

Q has offered to reveal the truth about the uncomfortable realities of our existence. I would love to tell you I've taken the red pill and never looked back, but that would be a lie. Taking the red pill means completely rejecting one's current view of the world and daring to accept an alternate reality—no matter how bizarre it may be. That proposition was a bridge too far for me. Rather than swallowing the red pill whole, I scraped off some of the outer coating and tasted it.

I happen to like my current view of the world even though I know much of what I believe isn't true. For me, holding onto certain things I currently believe is a matter of comfort, familiarity, and preservation of my sanity. What I've seen regarding the alternate narrative of the world greatly concerns, and in some ways, frightens me. It's one thing to arrive at the rooftop edge of a skyscraper you believe to be imaginary. It's another thing to step off the edge and find out. I prefer to learn the truth about our world gradually. As my mind is able to accept new realities, I incorporate them into my belief system.

There's another reason why I'm cautious. I've become acquainted with many people who say they've "taken the red pill." They distribute links to videos and articles that purport to expose deep secrets that the government and the media are hiding. Upon research, a large percentage of these claims cannot be verified. The narrative I currently hold may be false, but why would I replace it with one that may be equally false? The problem I have with taking someone else's "red pill" is that I need assurance that I'm not exchanging one delusion for another. If I were to find someone who could tell me the truth and provide evidence that it accurately represents reality, I would consider trading my view for theirs—and that is what I have found in Q.

Unlike many conspiracy theorists on the internet, Q has provided thousands of links to government documents and reputable, well-sourced articles that substantiate his claims. In addition, he has an uncanny ability to know about critical events weeks (sometimes months) before they happen. For these reasons, I've followed the trail of crumbs provided by Q, knowing that some degree of disinformation is necessary but also that reasonable proof is being provided along the way. For people like me, taking the red pill is a gradual experience. We immerse ourselves in the truth slowly, abandoning deceptions of the past one post at a time.

CHAPTER 9

Where We Go One, We Go All

ON SEVERAL OCCASIONS, Q HAS posted a link to the video trailer from the film *White Squall,* a fictionalized story based on actual events. In the movie, set in the 1960s, Jeff Bridges plays the skipper of a sailing ship bound for South America with a crew of inexperienced and undisciplined teenagers. The film explores the insecurities, fears, and failings of several boys. Each one, in turn, is offered help from the others. The ship has a bell with the inscription "Where We Go One, We Go All." The words become a rallying cry every time one of the boys overcomes a particular challenge.

One boy, Frank, cannot overcome his problems, which stem from an unhealthy relationship with his wealthy but manipulative father. After he kills a dolphin, Frank is removed from the ship by the skipper. The boat continues its journey but capsizes in a storm, and several crew members perish. Frank's father sees an opportunity for revenge and has the skipper investigated for incompetence. A hearing is convened to suspend the skipper's license, but the boys come to his defense, and the hearing ends without action being taken against him.

The skipper was tough but fair, and he knew how to motivate the boys. Sometimes they needed a pat on the back. Sometimes they needed a kick in the pants. He was adept at dishing out both. Q plays a role similar to that of the skipper. He encourages researchers and offers guidance, but he's not afraid to express his disappointment when they don't perform as expected.

In November of 2017, Q tried to get researchers to correctly decode his posts related to the stringer "Bunker Apple Yellow Sky." (That stringer is decoded in my first *Q Chronicles* book *Calm Before the Storm*.) Q gave anons many hints that were intended to help, but they still weren't seeing the big picture.

> Dec 9 2017
> Not understanding why the drops today aren't being understood.
> Expand your thinking.
> Important.
> Q

After reviewing hints that he had provided, Q told anons he may have overestimated their ability.

> Nov 21 2017
> ♦♦♦
> Who was the pilot of the plane?
> Bad actor?
> Who was the pilot of the helicopter?
> Green?
> What was countered?
> Who was on the ground (outside) shortly before the collision?
> Who was in the home shortly before the collision?
> Learn to read the map.
> We may have overestimated your ability.
> Q

An anon answered.

> **Spreadsheet Anon**
> >Who was the pilot of the plane?
> Green
> >What was countered?
> Unknown to us

>Who was on the ground (outside) shortly before the collision?
"Unnamed" Rothschild
>Who was in the home shortly before the collision?
Unknown to us now, was "dog grooming event"
>Learn to read the map.
trying really hard, is like herding kittens in here sometime
>We may have overestimated your ability.
you came to us for certain strengths but there are weaknesses
as well, some being exploited
not enough focus
answer the questions
build the big picture
break it back down
make memes for the normies to calm & educate
so we'll be ready for the Storm

Q responded.

Nov 21 2017
You are learning.
You needed a push.
Godspeed.
Q

In February of 2018, an anon pieced together several articles about the CIA's use of mind control. Q asked if any recent mass shooters had received therapy and encouraged anons to continue their research.

Feb 15 2018
Have any recent [shooters] received therapy in the past?
Be the autists we know you are.
You were chosen for a specific reason.
Q

Although Q experiences frustration from the researchers' inconsistent performance, he also expresses confidence that they're up to the task if they'll receive his instruction.

One may follow Q's posts on their own and benefit from the information provided. It isn't necessary to collaborate with others, but there are benefits to being part of a community. Q discusses hundreds of subjects. The average person is likely to have knowledge or firsthand experience in only a few of them. We can understand topics that we don't have knowledge of by learning from those who do. The beehive-like operation of the research board allows unlimited access to the work done by others. After getting accustomed to the way anons relate to one another, the community of Q researchers has become my second family.

Q helps us conduct research and encourages us to come to the truth on our own. As we do, we develop personalized narratives of historical and current events that differ from the ones held by others and those of the mainstream media. Because Q opposes the media's portrayal, he is attacked. If we oppose their narrative, we will also be attacked.

The press has slandered me in countless articles. I'm attacked daily on social media for sharing Q's messages. It would be easy to give up, but I receive daily encouragement from fellow researchers who tell me how valuable my contribution is or how my broadcasts have given them hope. When I know that my message is positively impacting others, it compels me to continue, despite the attacks. The success of Q's operation relies heavily on researchers receiving encouragement from one another.

> Feb 18 2019
> How can an entity known only as 'Q' (face-less, name-less, fame-less, etc.) begin to ask questions on 4ch (now 8ch) and build something of this magnitude?
> How can this same 'Q' entity garner such a massive amount of WW MSM [FAKE NEWS] attention [attacks]?
> ♦♦♦
> TRUST YOURSELF.
> TRUST THAT YOU ARE NOT ALONE.
> TRUST THAT THERE ARE GOOD PEOPLE RIGHT BESIDE YOU FIGHTING FOR WHAT WE KNOW TO BE RIGHT.
> GOD BLESS YOU ALL.
> WHERE WE GO ONE, WE GO ALL!
> Q

Decades ago, the owners of broadcast and print media controlled the public narrative, but social media changed all that. Today, mainstream reporters compete to have their voices heard on social media alongside non-mainstream influencers. To perpetuate the illusion that they still control the narrative, mainstream journalists portray Q's following as small and irrelevant, but nothing could be further from the truth. Tens of thousands of Q researchers are influencing millions of people around the world. Social media companies have banned our accounts because collectively, we're reaching people with the truth, and the media's lies are being rejected.

>
> Dec 2 2018 16:47:00 (EST)
> Power belongs to the people.
> You are what matters.
> All you needed was a spark to UNITE TOGETHER.
> They are scared.
> Think Fake News attacks [2nd only to POTUS himself].
> TOGETHER WE WIN.
> Trust yourself.
> Think for yourself.
> You are not alone.
> Open your heart and your mind.
> Where We Go One > We Go ALL!!!
> Q

CHAPTER 10

The Hunt for Red October

IN THIS CHAPTER, WE'LL EXPLORE the Q signature, "The Hunt for Red October," which first appeared in a post that we examined in the chapter "Iron Eagle." Consider the fact that both signatures are the titles of cold war films, and both appeared in the same post. This suggests that the signatures speak of topics that are related. Here is that post again for your review.

> Nov 20 2017 02:29:00
> What is a key?
> What is a key used for?
> What is a guard?
> What is a guard used for?
> Who unlocked the door of all doors?
> Was it pre-planned?
> Do you believe in coincidences?
> What is information?
> Who controls the release of information?
> WHO HAS ALL OF THE INFORMATION?
> Who disseminates information?

What is the MSM?
Who controls the MSM?
Who really controls the MSM?
Why are we made to believe the MSM are the only credible news sources?
Who controls the MSM?
Who really controls the MSM?
Why are we made to believe the MSM are the only credible news sources?
Why is this relevant?
Why are non MSM platforms cast as conspiracy and/or non-credible?
Why are non MSM platforms cast as conspiracy and/or non-credible?
What happens when an entity and/or individual accumulates power?
Define corruption.
Wealth = power.
Power = influence.
Influence = control.
Rinse and repeat.
What power of influence was recently discovered (specifically re: 2016 election)?
How much power of influence does Twitter, FB, Reddit, etc. have in influencing the minds of people?
Has the stranglehold of the MSM been diminished?
What is open source?
What has become blatantly obvious since the election of POTUS?
Why would they allow this (visibility) to occur?
Were they not prepared to counter?
What miscalculation occurred?
What opposite impact did this generate?
How did POTUS recognize and invert?
What happens when an entity and/or individual accumulates power?
Define corruption.
Define censorship.
Define 'controlled' censorship.

What action is Twitter taking effective mid-Dec?
What is the purpose of this action?
Possible test to understand public / gov't response?
(cont..)
When was this announced?
When did events in SA transpire?
Who controlled a large portion of Twitter stock?
Why is this relevant?
Define oppression.
Who controls the narrative?
Who really controls the narrative?
Who guards the narrative?
Does the MSM shelter and protect select 'party' members?
Does this protection insulate these 'party' members?
Who controls the narrative?
What laws were put in place to protect the MSM from lawsuits?
Who specifically passed this law?
What is immunity?
What prevents a news organization from simply 'making up sources & stories'?
What prevents a news organization from simply 'making up sources & stories'?
What previous SC ruling provided protection to reporters from having to reveal their 'confidential' source(s)?
How many people are unaware of the 'truth' due to the stranglehold?
How must people be made aware of an alternate reality?
What are crumbs (think H-wood/DC)
Define 'lead-in' (think play)?
What has been occurring recently?
The stage must be set.
Crumbs are easy to swallow.
What if Hugh Hefner was /a Clown In America?
What is a honeypot?
Define blackmail.
How could this be applied?
Fantasy land.
WHO HAS ALL OF THE INFORMATION?
No Such Agency.

> The hunter becomes the hunted.
> Operations underway.
> Operators active.
> Disinformation is real.
> Disinformation is necessary.
> Silent war (some gets out).
> The Great Awakening.
> Iron Eagle.
> Godfather III.
> The Hunt for Red October.
> Q

This post explained that the mainstream media had been controlled by the CIA, an agency that also controls powerful people through blackmail. The media and the CIA had, for decades, controlled the flow of information to the public, but that ended when people began using social media. Saudi princes tried to maintain control of the narrative by purchasing a majority of shares in social media companies, but their assets were frozen under the Trump administration, which removed their control. Information can be thought of as a key. President Trump has released information through Q that caused changes on the geopolitical stage.

On November 9th, 2017, Q posted the following message.

> Nov 12 2017
> Patriots don't sleep.
> 40,000ft. v. necessary to understand [US]/SA/global events.
> Paint the picture.
> Decrease altitude (we will not fly that high again).
> Higher the altitude greater the [risk] of conspiracy ST.
> Many cannot/will not swallow.
> What is No Such Agency - Q group?
> Who has clearance to full picture?
> Important.
> SIS is good.
> +++Adm R+++
> What agency is at war w/ Clowns In America?
> How does POTUS shift narrative?
> (New) Age of Enlightenment.

80% covert.
20% public.
What has occurred over [th]e last several months?
C-info leaks?

♦♦♦

Q explained that we are currently engaged in an information war. The NSA (No Such Agency) and President Trump are battling the CIA and bad actors in the deep state. The key to the deep state's success is secrecy. Trump and the NSA plan to defeat them by disclosing information about their corruption. Q explained that twenty percent of the information the NSA has would be disclosed while eighty percent would remain classified.

On December 18th, 2017, Q began posting on the 8chan board /cbts/. On the 19th, he posted the following message.

> Dec 19 2017
> Board owner, mods, and other patriots:
> Sincere thanks for all that you do.
> You are true heroes.
> Long overdue - my apologies.
> There will be a day (within the next few months) that a scary but safe personalized message finds its way to you on multiple platforms recognizing your contributions.
> We thank you for your service.
> Godspeed,
> Q

An anon apologized for causing a problem related to Q's tripcode during the migration to the new board.

> **Anonymous**
> Thank you Sir...
> Sorry for the Trip mess up earlier...

Q responded.

> Safety first.
> We have the USSS, NSA, and DHS, also protecting this message.

No random IP needed (though we can implement at a moments notice).
Godspeed,
Q

Less than an hour later, Q posted again.

Dec 19 2017 23:10:31
SEA_TO_SHINING_SEA
DIRECT: CODE 234 SEC: B1-3
DIRECT: CODE 299 SEC: F19-A
[C   P   19]
Show the World Our Power.
RED_OCTOBER >
Q

The first thing I would point out is that this post contains the stringer "RED_OCTOBER" but not the entire phrase "The Hunt for Red October." Next, I would draw your attention to number 19, which happened to be the date of the post. Also note the letters C and P. When I examined the posts between December 19th and December 21st, I noticed that Q referred to how much information would be made public and how much would remain classified. I wondered if perhaps the letter "C" in the stringer in brackets stood for "classified" and "P" stood for "public." Two minutes after he posted this message, Q posted again.

Dec 19 2017 23:12:54
SWEET DREAMS.
P_pers: Public (not private).
NATSEC_19384z_A_DT-approve
Q

Note the stringer "P_pers" in the post above. Q has used this stringer on many occasions. We've learned that this is how he indicates that a message was sent from the President (P), personally (pers) to the board. The subject of the post was the ongoing discussion of how much information would be kept private (classified) and how much would be made public. The post closes with a stringer about Donald Trump (DT) approving something related to National Security (NATSEC).

The next day, December 20th, President Trump signed an Executive Order authorizing the U.S. Treasury Department to freeze the assets of individuals and organizations found to be involved in corruption, human rights abuse, and human trafficking. The following day, an anon posted the message below after seeing a tweet from *ABC News* about the Executive Order.

> **Anonymous** • Dec 21 2017
> FOUND IT!!! HOLY SHIT!
> https://twitter.com/ABCPolitics/status/943866651803611136

Q responded, saying that the President had changed his mind about greater transparency regarding the exposure of corruption. He indicated that the signal of the change had been posted two days earlier, on the 19th.

> We were inspired by anons here to make our efforts more public.
> Find the exchange 2 days ago.
> Feel proud!
> Q

An anon said he believed the Executive Order had to do with greater public disclosure.

> **Anonymous** • Dec 21 2017
> Multiple people were asking Q to make things more public. RE: calling for full disclosure

Q responded, saying the President was listening to them and honored their request.

> Dec 21 2017
> Correct exchange.
> Anon(s) changed our mind re: Private / Public.
> We are listening.
> Highest priorty.
> Have faith.
> Q

Some decisions are made by President Trump and Q without considering the feelings of anons. Other decisions take into account our desires. On January 13th, 2018, Q confirmed that the decision was made to declassify forty percent of the information they had, while keeping only sixty percent secret.

```
Jan 13 2018
[MONDAY]
Next Week - BIGGER.
PUBLIC.
We LISTENED [20/80 />/ 40/60].
Q
```

In February of 2018, Q asked why he was allowed to continue his operation and why the FBI was not investigating him.

```
Feb 11 2018
Think BDT NYC 'attempt' & Barlow.
Not stated for verification of credibility.
Why are we still here given foreknowledge of events?
No FBI investigation into this?
Impossible to locate?
Less than 10.
Who are we talking to?
Since Clown takedown of black_ops loc/public exposure what has changed here?
Expand your thinking.
This is not a game.
RED_OCTOBER.
Q
```

The abbreviations BDT NYC pertain to Q's foreknowledge of a pipe bomb detonated in New York City (NYC) by a would-be terrorist from Bangladesh (BDT). "Barlow" refers to John Perry Barlow and Q's post saying heart attacks can be deadly one week before Barlow was found dead from a heart attack. Q is difficult to locate because, in his words, less than ten people can confirm his identity.

The signature "Red October" seems to pertain to the disclosure of information, but it appears in posts about other subjects.

An anon asked Q about the meaning of the signature.

> **Anonymous** • Feb 11 2018
> I would like to inquire of Q (with highest respect) whether RED_OCTOBER refers to
> 1) the fictional submarine whose torpedo homed in on itself and destroyed itself
> Or
> 2) the [RED OCTOBER] [Красный Октябрь] cyberespionage malware discovered in October 2012-January 2013. It operated worldwide for up to 5 years before its discovery. It sent info ranging from diplomatic secrets to personal information, including from mobile devices. Red October was termed an advanced cyberespionage campaign intended to target diplomatic, governmental and scientific research organizations worldwide.
> or
> 3) Something else

Q responded.

> Future news will highlight.
> Note "The Hunt For" was dropped.
> Details matter.
> Q

It is not unusual for one of Q's signatures to change over time. Although Q initially used the full title of the Tom Clancy novel, *The Hunt for Red October*, the signature was modified. "The Hunt for" was dropped. Just after midnight, on March 6th, 2018, Q posted some hints.

> Mar 6 2018 00:39:55
> Learn double meanings.
> News unlocks MAP.
> Why is STEEL so important?
> Expand your thinking.
> https://www.cia.gov/library/readingroom/docs/CIA-RDP80-00810A004000690005-7.pdf
> Q

Q's post suggested a recent news story would unlock a double meaning for the phrase "Red October." The post contained a link to a document hosted on the CIA website. The document dated April 28, 1954, explained how the Red October Steel plant in Stalingrad, Russia, was destroyed during World War II, but was later rebuilt. Q asked why steel was so important and told anons to expand their thinking.

An anon responded.

> **Anonymous** • Mar 6 2018
> ♦♦♦
> RED OCTOBER STEEL PLANT

Q replied.

> Why was 'The HUNT For' removed?
> Expand your thinking.
> Not related to $ or trade.
> The MAP has EVERYTHING.
> News / Tweets unlock the MAP.
> Q

An anon replied.

> **Anonymous** • Mar 6 2018
> Why is steel so important? Let's look where steel -was- produced in our country. These cities are blue strongholds, still, and many are located around areas of poor minorities, since mills closed and wealth left the area. If Trump brings these people back in to work he can effectively eliminate blue-collar/poor black democrat areas.
> AMERICAN STEEL

Another anon wrote:

> **Anonymous** • Mar 6 2018
> Steel is important to Defense Dept for weapons, planes ships, tanks, satellites etc., and for GNP output such as automobile plants, and steel is important for infrastructure rebuilding.

Q responded to both anons.

> What if the steel used for military-grade projects was made-inferior by our enemies as a method to weaken?
> What if Hussein knew and authorized?
> Renegade.
> How many Marines volunteered to serve Hussein during his term?
> Why?
> What if his name we don't say organized the deal?
> The US taxpayer subsidizes the WORLD.
> AMERICA has been sold to the highest bidder.
> AMERICA has been weakened on purpose.
> The depths of their TREASON is unimaginable.
> Pure EVIL.
> HELL on earth - HRC victory.
> Q

According to Q, politicians knew that steel was being weakened, but it played into their plan of weakening the United States so it could ultimately be destroyed and made part of a borderless, global community. Q implied that Barack Obama, John McCain, and Hillary Rodham Clinton (HRC) helped facilitate the plan.

Later that day, Q posted a link to a *Reuters* news article.

> Mar 6 2018 10:56:18 (EST)
> Do you believe in coincidences?
> Only the beginning.
> https://mobile.reuters.com/article/amp/idUSKBN1GH2SM?__twitter_impression=true
> Q

The article reported an admission from the CEO of Japan's third-largest steel producer, Kobe Steel Ltd, that the company had provided steel with falsely stated specifications to about 500 customers around the globe. As suggested by Q, this recent news story unlocked new meaning.

Two days later, on March 8th, 2018, President Trump announced that he would impose tariffs on foreign steel and aluminum. During the press conference, Trump made a very obvious Q hand gesture. Q posted a link to a video of the announcement and then reposted an anon's comment.

> Mar 8 2018
> Q HAND GESTURE WAT

Regarding the tariffs, an anon made this observation.

> **Anonymous** • Mar 8 2018
> Was necessary. China produces 10x as much steel as US. What if war breaks out?
> Matter of national security, geopolitics ...to prevent war, peace trough strength.

Q responded.

> + deliberate performance issues to impact military / infrastructure.
> We were sold out.
> You have so much more than you know.
> Q

According to Q, elected officials knowingly allowed steel used in military applications to be weakened to damage the nation's defense capabilities.

In September of 2018, Justice Brett Kavanaugh was nominated to fill a vacancy on the Supreme Court. During the confirmation process, he suffered personal attacks against his character. Q linked his confirmation fight to the signature Red October.

> Sep 27 2018 22:47:55
> Justice K confirmation
> Goodbye, Mr. Rosenstein
> DECLAS
> POTUS Alert-Test
> RED OCTOBER?
> Q

Rod Rosenstein served as Deputy Attorney General from 2017-2019. Q indicated in other posts that Rosenstein would be leaving the Justice

Department because he was compromised. Nine minutes after the previous post, Q connected the signature phrase Red October to the 2018 mid-term elections.

```
Sep 27 2018  22:56:59
RED OCTOBER>>>
MIDTERM ELECTIONS
RED WAVE OR RED TSUNAMI?
FIGHT!
FIGHT!
FIGHT!
Q
```

The Republican party is the party of Donald Trump and the party's color is red. An election favoring Republicans would be considered a "red wave," while one that favored Democrats would be a "blue wave."

The next day, Q elaborated on the significance of the 2018 election.

```
Sep 28 2018
D's Playbook (Midterm E):
We will impeach Justice K (ZERO corroborating evidence
and ALL factual witnesses provided by accuser ALL DENIED
ALLEGATIONS) should we take control in NOV.
LIBERAL LEFT LUNACY [BAIT].
These people are EVIL, SICK, & STUPID.
You are watching/witnessing the systematic destruction of the
OLD GUARD.
OLD GUARD  >>>  POWER TO THE PEOPLE
RED OCTOBER.
Q
```

Q explained that if Democrats won control of Congress in the 2018 elections, they would set up the impeachment of Justice Kavanaugh, despite the fact that purported victims and witnesses denied the allegations against him. The old guard is being removed, and power is being restored to the people.

On September 30th, just before the election, Q+ posted about Red October. (Recall that it is believed that messages signed by Q+ are sent by President Trump.)

Sep 30 2018
RED OCTOBER
STAY TUNED AND WATCH!
Q+

On November 6th, 2018, the midterm elections were held. The following day, President Trump asked for the resignation of then-Attorney General Jeff Sessions. The move created controversy as Sessions had recused himself from the investigation of Trump by Special Counsel Robert Mueller. The recusal by Sessions left Rod Rosenstein to supervise Mueller's investigation. Those who opposed Trump repeatedly warned that he would remove Rosenstein. Such a move was considered to be a "red line" he had better not cross. With the resignation of Sessions, the media began fretting about the removal of Rosenstein. Q posted the following message in response.

Nov 7 2018
RED LINE ON THE ANNIVERSARY OF RED OCTOBER?
NOW WHAT ARE THE ODDS OF THAT?
Q

The Bolshevik revolution of 1917 (also known as the October Revolution or Red October) is celebrated on November 7th. Q suggested that Rod Rosenstein participated in a plot to trap President Trump in an investigation designed to keep him under public suspicion of committing a crime. The investigation limited his effectiveness during his first term in office. Whoever replaced Jeff Sessions as Attorney General would likely not be recused, and they would assume oversight of Mueller's investigation. William Barr became the new Attorney General. Not long afterward, Mueller's investigation ended without charges being filed against Trump, and Rod Rosenstein left the Department of Justice.

These are just a few of the connections to the signature The Hunt for Red October. There are others, and I would encourage you to spend time exploring them.

CHAPTER 11
Question and Answer

ON OCCASION, Q ALLOWS TIME to answer questions from anons. While disinformation is sometimes provided in Q's posts, this would seem to be a time set aside to take questions that can be answered truthfully. Q's first question and answer session was held on April 19, 2018. Below are the questions and answers from that session. For clarity, I have included the words "Question" and "Answer," though these words were not in the original posts. (Where the question or answer is unclear, an explanation will be given.)

> Apr 19 2018 21:13:29
> Q&A
> 5 min.
> Q

Anon's Question:
HRC v"dark web" video fake news???

Answer:
Fake.

We control.
Q

In a prior post, Q referenced a video of Hillary Clinton that could prove embarrassing if it were released. A video had surfaced purporting to show her engaged in horrific acts. Q confirmed the video was fake and that his team had control of the real video.

Anon's Question:
Federal Reserve ending?

Answer:
Structure.
Q

Many people anticipated that Donald Trump would end the Federal Reserve. Q suggested its power would be reined in by restructuring.

Anon's Question:
When will we find out about Seth Rich and Las Vegas??

Answer:
SR connect to DNC.
MS_13.
JA.
Why did the D's push legal rep on family?
June ETA.
Q

Q has often suggested that Seth Rich was the source of the 2016 leak of DNC emails to Julian Assange (JA) and Wikileaks. He maintains that Rich was murdered my members of the gang MS-13, and that Democrats pushed the family to hire an attorney who steered them away from the truth. Q anticipated action on Assange's extradition in June of 2018, but it has been delayed by U.K. authorities. As of April 2023, reports say Australia's Prime Minister Anthony Albanese is seeking a diplomatic solution.

Anon's Question:
Will Europe really be broken from its chains too?

Answer:
WW.
Q

Saudi Arabia was the first nation to be set free from the control of bad actors. The United States is second. Other nations in Europe and Asia will follow. (WW is usually decoded as worldwide.)

Anon's Question:
Will election fraud be revealed soon???

Answer:
Yes, midterms are safe.
Watch CA.
Q

Q indicated that election fraud will be revealed, that the 2018 midterm elections were safe, and that anons should keep an eye on California (CA). On September 19th, 2018, Q hosted a second question and answer session.

Anon's Question:
Trudeau, ANYTHING?
owl

Answer:
Billionaire(s) 187.
FVEY
Safety House Build.
U1 Funnel >> Canada >> X
Q

Q indicated that Canadian billionaires Barry and Honey Sherman were connected to Prime Minister Trudeau. They were murdered (187) in their home in 2017. On December 23, 2017, *The New York Post* reported that just days before they died, the Shermans' attorney filed documents in court in an attempt to quash a government investigation into allegations that lobbying rules were violated when they hosted a $1,100-a-plate fundraising dinner at their home for Justin Trudeau in 2015. The murder remains unsolved, and in January 2023, the couple's son Jonathan offered a reward of $35 million for any tip that leads to the arrest of his parents' killer.

Q has implicated Canada and other nations in the Five Eyes (FVEY) intelligence sharing agreement as co-conspirators in the 2016 surveillance of the Trump campaign. According to Q, the sale of the North American Company Uranium One to the Russian company Rosatom helped funnel uranium from Canada to rogue nations who used it in the development of covert nuclear weapons programs.

Anon's Question:
Flynn exonerated soon?

Answer:
In the end, all will be right.
Patriots protect Patriots.
Q

Anon's Question:
Are they going to continue to hide behind Sexual misconduct or will the truth come out?

Answer:
Sexual misconduct is the 'public shelter' to accept resignation.
Watch those announcing 2020 P running.
"You cannot attack a political opponent"
None are protected.
None are safe.
Q

Q has suggested that sexual harassment is the publicly acceptable story under which corrupt politicians will resign, rather than having even worse crimes revealed. It is accepted practice not to bring criminal charges against a Presidential candidate after they announce their intent to run for office. Some 2020 Presidential candidates may have chosen to run in order to provide cover from investigation of their crimes.

At the time of this post, CodeMonkey (/CM/) was the website administrator for 8chan. One of his duties was keeping Q's board operational. Because question and answer is a popular activity (everyone wants to have their question answered by Q) it tests the system's resources.

Question and Answer

Q posted a request for more resources:

/CM/ pls divert more resources/bandwidth into board.
Q

Anon's Question:
Q, Was the Pentagon hit by plane on 911

Answer:
Yes
Q

Anon's Question:
Are we alone?
Roswell?

Answer:
No.
Highest classification.
Consider the vastness of space.
Q

Apparently, life is known to exist outside our planet. It seems that a space program was developed some time ago (perhaps with the capacity for interstellar travel), but it has been kept secret under the highest government classification.

Anon's Question:
Was moving the date back on POTUS FEMA "Presidential Alert" significant?

Answer:
Due to K confirmation push.
Hand in hand.
[RR] stand down due to K conf.
Q

In 2018, the Federal Emergency Management Agency (FEMA) approved a new system that would allow the President to send a text message to every phone in the United States. A test of the system was scheduled for Thursday, September 20th, 2018, at 2:18 pm ET, but it was postponed until October 3rd and confirmed by FEMA in the following tweet:

> **FEMA** (from its Twitter account)
> Due to severe weather across much of the East Coast and ongoing response efforts, the national emergency alert test has been postponed to the backup date of Oct. 3, 2018 at 2:18 PM EDT.
>
> If you have questions about the test, visit the FAQ at http://fema.gov/emergency-alert-test.
> 9:44 AM - 17, September, 2018

According to Q, there was another purpose for the postponement. It forced then-Deputy Attorney General Rod Rosenstein [RR] to stand down regarding an unknown action related to the nomination of Supreme Court Justice Brett Kavanaugh (K), whose controversial confirmation process ended on October 6, 2018, when the U.S. Senate confirmed him.

> /CM/ pls confirm ASAP resource upgrade.
> Tracking 330,000 IPs which is causing extreme lag.
> Q

Q said there were 330,000 users online and asked CodeMonkey to confirm that more resources were being diverted to the board.

> **Anon's Question:**
> Q, Did NASA fake the moon landings? Have we been to the moon since then? Are there secret space programs? Is this why the Space Force was created?
>
> **Answer:**
> False, moon landings are real.
> Programs exist that are outside of public domain.
> Q

Q confirmed that the moon landings were real and implied that unacknowledged programs exist that are related to space exploration.

Anon's Comment:
>we're DEF being attack'd
Anon's Comment:
No, we are ddosing ourselves with over 330,000 IPs

Answer:
412,000 now.
Q

An anon said the board was under attack. A second anon responded that the board wasn't under attack, but that anons were causing a disruption similar to a DDoS attack. A distributed denial-of-service (DDoS) attack is a malicious attempt to disrupt the normal traffic of a server with a flood of internet traffic. It creates a traffic jam of sorts that overwhelms the resources of the system. Anons weren't creating a malicious attack, but the system was simply lagging trying to handle 330,00 users. Q replied that there were now 412,000 users online. The session ended when the board could no longer handle the traffic.

On December 12, 2018, Q hosted a third question and answer session.

Anon's Question:
How do you know the future?

Answer:
Control.
Q

Q has jokingly suggested that he uses time travel, but when asked directly how he is able to anticipate future events, he explained that it's because he has a degree of control over how and when they happen. (One would infer that this control comes by virtue of his relationship to President Trump.)

Anon's Question:
Is Seth alive?

Answer:
No.
Q

Internet rumors at the time claimed that Seth Rich was alive. Q confirmed he was not.

Anon's Question:
What were in the envelopes ???

Answer:
Our promise to 'counter'.
Q

An explanation of the envelope question can be found in chapter 14.

Anon's Question:
Is there a plan in place for AFTER trump?

Answer:
Yes.
Q

Anon's Question:
Will voter fraud be exposed before January?

Answer:
No.
2019 push Voter ID based on verifiable intel (fraud).
2020+ safeguarded.
Q

An anon asked if voter fraud would be exposed before January 2019. Q said it would not, and that President Trump would make a push to get states to implement voter ID laws based on evidence of fraud. According to Q, elections after 2020 would be safeguarded against fraud.

Anon's Question:
Is JFK Jr alive?

Answer:
No.
Q

In the summer of 2018, many people became convinced—and some still continue to talk about the possibility—that John F. Kennedy Jr. survived a plane crash, and is presently alive, living under a pseudonym. However, Q confirmed that he is not alive.

Anon's Question:
What about Snowden?

Answer:
Negotiating for return.
Traitor.
Mission to harm NSA.
Q

Edward Snowden is widely hailed as a champion of free speech and transparency regarding government surveillance. However, Q has highlighted the fact that Snowden first worked for the CIA and was sent into the NSA on a mission to discredit the agency. Snowden's leak of the tools PRISM and XKeyscore were intended to harm the NSA and give the CIA the upper hand in their inter-agency battle for information dominance. Negotiations were underway to extradite Snowden to the United States.

Anon's Question:
Q is JA stateside?

Answer:
No.
Q

In 2018, people some claimed that Julian Assange (JA) had secretly been extradited to the United States. Q confirmed he had not.

Anon's Question:
Is this a stress test?

Answer:
Yes.
Added server(s)/bandwidth improved performance.
Q

One purpose for question-and-answer sessions is to test the capacity of the system under extreme conditions.

Anon's Question
Q - Should we be prepping for some kind of shutdown?

Answer:
No. Reports of 'power grid' attacks (6 mo prep) should be disregarded.
While attacks do occur, we are safeguarded by a 'Black Eye'.
Q

Q said that at the time, there was no significant threat of a widespread takedown of the power grid. (Theories have been proposed as to what the "Black Eye" is but none have been confirmed.)

Anon's Comment:
0 delta
Q/POTUS

Answer:
Not intended.
Separated by 2.
Q

During the question-and-answer session, an anon noticed that Q and President Trump posted at the same time, causing a "zero delta," but Q replied that it was unintentional.

Anon's Question:
Is internet infrastructure being safeguarded to prevent shut down?

Answer:
NSA ability to overreach hosts possible.
Q

Many people have become concerned about the possibility of a widespread internet outage. Q suggested that military intelligence (specifically the

NSA) has the ability to counter a potential shutdown at the internet hosting level.

Anon's Question:
Will Flotus confirm anything on Hannity tonight?

Answer:
Only her beauty and love of country.
Q

An anon wondered if then-first lady (FLOTUS) Melania Trump would make a surprise disclosure of information on Sean Hannity's show that night, but Q said she would not.

Anon's Question:
Q: Do we have the gold?

Answer:
Yes.
Gold shall destroy FED.
Q

Apparently, Donald Trump's long-term plan to deal with the Federal Reserve has to do with a return to a gold-standard of some kind.

Anon's Comment:
Q is talking about GOOG's 10-Q filing with the SEC. My assumption would be for their 3/31/19 or 6/30/19 10-Q filing.

Answer:
Assumption correct.
10k YE.
2019 1 + 2 should be closely evaluated.
Help will be provided.
Senate to investigate 2019.
Q

The question was in reference to a request by Q the previous day for anons to look into Google's financial statements for evidence of nefarious activities. Forms 10-Q and 10-K are financial reports that must be submitted by all public companies to the Securities and Exchange Commission (SEC). Form 10-Q is filed quarterly. Form 10-K is submitted annually. This was the previous day's post by Q:

Dec 11 2018 23:42:39 (EST)
GOOG (upcoming) financial statements should receive extra scrutiny [10-Q].
Follow the money.
Help will be provided.
Q

The above post was a follow-up to this one:

Dec 11 2018 23:33:44 (EST)
https://motherboard.vice.com/en_us/article/gy7mnx/google-ceo-says-no-plans-to-launch-dragonfly-chinese-search-engine-sundar-pichai
Google CEO Says No Plan to 'Launch' Censored Search Engine in China"
How do you cover your tracks?
Start a FIRE.
GOOG says NO PLAN TO LAUNCH.......
What if GOOG already gave access to China?
CHINA launch?
WILL CHINA BE ANNOUNCING A STATE-FUNDED & STATE-MADE NEW SEARCH ENGINE IN THE COMING MONTHS?
The FIRE that brought down GOOGLE.
Q

Citizens continued to have concerns about corrupt elections. An anon brought up the subject in the next question from December 12th:

Anon's Question:
Will voter fraud in CA ever be brought to light?

Answer:
Yes. "Watch CA" was deliberate.
Q

Apparently, there are plans to expose voter fraud in the state of California (CA), according to Q.

Anon's Question:
Just to shut the Flat Earthers up Q, Is the Earth flat?

Answer:
No.
Q

Anon's Question:
Is Gitmo going to be used for US citizens (cabal)?

Answer:
(3) detention centers being prepped.
Monitor funding.
Q

It seems that if one monitors the funding disbursements of the U.S. Bureau of Prisons, they might find evidence of three detention centers being prepared to incarcerate criminal elites. It is not clear if this would be in addition to or instead of their detainment at Guantanamo Bay Naval Air Station (GITMO).

Anon's Question:
Q, please tell us who or what the Wizards and Warlocks are.

Answer:
'Guardians' of intelligence.
Q

When the website received more traffic than it could handle, Q notified anons that the question and answer session was over.

/End
Stress test failed.
Q

CHAPTER 12

Follow the Pen

Q PROVIDES SEVERAL LINES OF evidence to support the claim that he is an intelligence insider close to Donald Trump. That evidence includes photographs of a pen that is believed to be owned by Trump. The first such photo was posted on December 12th, 2017.

> Dec 12 2017 17:03:32 (EST)
> Exec_y.png
> Merry Christmas.
> Q

The blurred picture posted by Q showed a dark brown pen and a white sheet of paper (or perhaps a folder) embossed with the Presidential Seal. When the image is rotated 90 degrees counterclockwise so that the Presidential Seal is in its normal orientation, a series of numbers in dark ink can be seen below the seal that are blurred and partially obscured by the pen. The numbers 1 and 3 can be made out. It's possible that to the right of the number 3 is the number 8. An internet search for identical images returned no results, suggesting that the image may have been an original. A nearly identical pen to the one in the picture is found in the Montblanc Starwalker Extreme series. Image file names are sometimes relevant. The name of the attached image file was Exec_y. It's possible that the white sheet of paper was a Presidential Executive Order. The letter Y sometimes indicates "yes."

Ten minutes after Q posted the pen image, President Trump tweeted a Hanukkah greeting.

> **Donald J. Trump** (from his Twitter account):
> Wishing all of those celebrating #Hanukkah around the world a happy and healthy eight nights in the company of those they love. http://45.wh.gov/XpFsZu
> 5:13 PM - 12 Dec 2017

The tweet by President Trump mentioned "eight nights." Coincidentally, Executive Order 13818 was signed by the President eight days (or nights) later, on Dec 20th, 2017. That order authorized the U.S. Treasury to block the assets of individuals and organizations involved in human trafficking, human rights abuse, or corruption. In summary: Trump tweeted about eight nights. Eight days later, he issued an Executive Order. Q posted what may have been a photo of the Executive Order 10 minutes before the President's tweet, and consecutive numbers visible in the image are found in the Executive Order.

Eighteen minutes after the President's tweet, Q posted again, drawing attention to the time interval between his previous post with a timestamp of 17:03 and the President's tweet ten minutes later at 17:13 (5:13 pm).

> Dec 12 2017 17:31:52 (EST)
> Timestamp [Q] post [:03] against POTUS' Tweet [:13].
> [10]
> No coincidences.
> Q

On December 23rd, at 3:22 pm (15:22 military time), Q asked anons to search his posts for references to former FBI Deputy Director Andrew McCabe, sometimes called #2 because he was second in command at the bureau.

> Dec 23 2017 15:22:21 (EST)
> SEARCH crumbs: [#2]

Who is #2?
No deals.
Q

Five minutes later, President Trump tweeted about Andrew McCabe.

Donald J. Trump (from his Twitter account):
How can FBI Deputy Director Andrew McCabe, the man in charge, along with leakin' James Comey, of the Phony Hillary Clinton investigation (including her 33,000 illegally deleted emails) be given $700,000 for wife's campaign by Clinton Puppets during investigation?
3:27:05 PM - 23 Dec 2017

An anon posted a screencap of President Trump's tweet and noted there was a seven-minute difference between the tweet and Q's post about #2.

Anonymous • Dec 23 2017 16:46:08 (EST)
9A47B7E5-08EF-42B2-A720-374C8B587981.jpg
Confirms Q posted about McCabe 7 mins prior to trumps first tweet about McCabe today

Q confirmed the discovery but noted the time interval was actually five minutes. He told anons they were missing ten minute and fifteen minute intervals between Q and Trump posts from the past.

Dec 23 2017 16:49:11 (EST)
5 minutes.
Missing 10 marker from past.
Missing 15 marker from past.
Timestamps have meaning.
Q

Three minutes later, Q posted again.

Dec 23 2017 16:52:31 (EST)
Graphics should be in same time zone.
Delta relevant.
[5]Today

[10]Past
[15]Past
Q

In the above post, Q asked anons to create side-by-side graphics to compare his post's timestamps and those of the President's tweets. Specific time intervals (deltas) were mentioned, including an interval that day of five minutes, and past intervals of ten minutes and fifteen minutes. The ten-minute interval between the first pen photo posted by Q and the President's Hanukkah tweet on December 12th was the missing ten-minute interval Q had mentioned.

On January 6th, 2018, an anon posted a side-by-side graphic showing the five-minute and ten-minute intervals between Q's posts and tweets by the President.

Then, Q responded by posting another photo of the same pen resting on a wood desk.

Jan 6 2018 16:14:22 (EST)
PEN_.png
Look familiar?
Note the desk.
Where is everyone this weekend?
GOD BLESS.
Q

President Trump happened to be at Camp David that weekend meeting with advisers. Once again, an internet search for the photo returned no matching images.

On January 24th, 2018, Q posted another photo of the Montblanc pen.

Jan 24 2018 15:50:32 (EST)
RTM.png

This time, the pen was lying on a sheet of paper. Although the image was slightly blurred, one can see the Presidential Seal on it. (The file name was RTM. I have no theory as to what RTM might mean, and Q did not confirm any guesses.)

Three months later, Q posted the following message.

> Apr 19 2018 16:54:59 (EST)
> We have everything.
> How can we use what we know?
> How do you 'legally' inject/make public/use as evidence?
> What are you witnessing unfold?
> Trust the plan.
> Q

Q has alluded to the possibility that he works for (or is in some way connected to) the National Security Agency. The NSA collects all electronically transmitted communications, including evidence of crimes. It's one thing to have access to incriminating evidence. The question is how one might make that information available to the public or have it admitted as evidence in court. A law enforcement agent with a warrant can obtain data collected by the NSA. Q highlights open source information of which the public is not aware.

Nine minutes later, Q posted again.

> Apr 19 2018 17:03:58
> EO.
> Treason.
> Update.
> Read.
> Study the EOs.
> Follow the 'pen'.
> EOs post 'pen' pics.
> Connect.
> Learn.
> SKY Event.
> Q

Q connected the pen images to Presidential Executive Orders (EOs). The photos seem to foretell important Executive Orders that are not public when the pen images are posted. By studying them after they're published, we learn about the President's plan to deal with corruption. There has not yet been a definitive decode for "SKY Event."

On May 10th, 2018, Q posted another photo of the Montblanc pen.

> May 10 2018 20:49:00 (EST)
> DOJNUNESRELEASE.png

A sheet of paper is visible in this image that had the Presidential Seal on it. The paper is inside a dark brown portfolio like the one the President uses to hold an Executive Order. The pen is resting beside the portfolio. The file name DOJNUNESRELEASE suggests that an order was prepared by the President authorizing the declassification and release of a memo by then-House Intelligence Chair Devin Nunes regarding FISA abuse by the Obama administration. In the lower right corner of the image, a few letters of text are visible but not enough to know what the document says.

About an hour later, Q posted again.

> May 10 2018 21:43:20
> Fellow Patriots:
> What you are about to learn should not only scare you, but intensify your resolve to take back control [Freedom]. The information that will become public will further demonstrate the criminal & corrupt [pure evil] abuse of power that the Hussein administration undertook in joint efforts w/ domestic and foreign dignitaries. The snowball has begun rolling - there is no stopping it now. D5.
> Stay the course and trust the plan.
> Protective measures are in place.
> Remain BRAVE.
> We knew this day would come.
> https://www.youtube.com/watch?v=G2qlXXafxCQ
> United We Stand (WW).
> WWG1WGA.
> We FIGHT.
> Conspiracy no more.
> Q

Q and Donald Trump intend to expose the corrupt acts of the Obama administration. Once the process begins, it will snowball, and nothing can stop it. The North American Avalanche Danger Scale rates the severity of avalanches from D1-D5, with D5 being the most severe. Metaphorically speaking, D5 is a warning from Q that the corrupt political establishment will suffer massive damage.

On May 16th, 2018, Ohio Representative Jim Jordan tweeted a request for declassification and release of documents from the DOJ and FBI related to FISA surveillance of the Trump campaign.

> **Jim Jordan** (from his Twitter account):
> It's high time for transparency. The DOJ and FBI have continually and repeatedly thwarted congressional oversight. We're asking @realDonaldTrump to direct the Attorney General to give us the documents—because the American people deserve answers.
> 11:34 AM - 16 May 2018

Q posted a link to Jim Jordan's tweet.

> Q !4pRcUAOIBE
> May 16 2018 13:45:50
> Follow the pen.
> Already written?
> Letters left visible to match.
> https://mobile.twitter.com/Jim_Jordan/status/996821093146120192
> WWG1WGA!
> Q

According to Q, the Executive Order authorizing declassification had already been written, and he had posted a photo of it, leaving letters visible that would serve as proof. Please note Q's tripcode in the above post. Q had been using the tripcode Q !4pRcUAOIBE since May 8th, 2018. It will become relevant shortly.

Three days later, on May 19th, President Trump tweeted the following.

> **Donald J. Trump** (from his Twitter account):
> If the FBI or DOJ was infiltrating a campaign for the benefit of another campaign, that is a really big deal. Only the release or review of documents that the House Intelligence Committee

(also, Senate Judiciary) is asking for can give the conclusive answers. Drain the Swamp!
2:27 PM - 19 May 2018

Q posted a screenshot of the President's tweet along with the following message and a separate message in the form of a new tripcode.

NowC@mesTHEP@in—-23!!!
May 19 2018 17:03:54 (EST)
20180519_222857.png
They thought it was coming yesterday.
They were wrong.
Follow the pen.
Q

It seems the President's enemies were expecting the release of documents on the 18th. Please note that Q was logged in under a different tripcode in the above post: NowC@mesTHEP@in—-23!!!

Q posted three minutes later to let anons know he was changing his tripcode again.

Q !4pRcUAOIBE
May 19 2018 17:06:20 (EST)
TRIP CHANGE
Q

One minute later, Q posted again with a new tripcode.

Q !CbboFOtcZs
May 19 2018 17:07:06 (EST)
Updated.
Q

Five seconds later, an unknown person hacked Q's previous tripcode and posted.

Q !4pRcUAOIBE
May 19 2018 17:07:11
Reeeee

One second later, a person using the same tripcode posted this message.

> Q !4pRcUAOIBE
> May 19 2018 17:07:12
> Password exposed?

Three minutes later, Q posted again under his new tripcode.

> Q !CbboFOtcZs
> May 19 2018 17:10:28 (EST)
> Mistake or on purpose?
> Q

An anon responded.

> **Anonymous** • May 19 2018 17:13:43 (EST)
> You knew when you set that trip, that the PAIN would be delivered "—-23!!!"
> More evidence of foreknowledge.

Q replied.

> May 19 2018 17:17:19 (EST)
> I'd watch the news that day.
> Q

It appears that Q intentionally allowed his tripcode to be hacked and when it was, a message to bad actors was provided in it. Theories have been proposed about the tripcode (NowC@mesTHEP@in—-23!!!) but Q has not confirmed any speculation about the meaning of it.

Q notified the board owner (BO), and CodeMonkey (CM), the site administrator, that his tripcode (hash) was secure.

> May 19 2018 17:23:33 (EST)
> CM/BO/:
> IP hash release OK.
> Proves same throughout.
> We control [utility].
> Q

Eighteen minutes later, Q posted an image of the Montblanc pen along with a link to a tweet by President Trump.

May 19 2018 17:41:54 (EST)
FTP.png
https://twitter.com/realDonaldTrump/status/997951982467014656

In the photo, the pen sits atop a dark brown folder that appears to have an Executive Order inside. Part of the document is visible, showing a portion of the President's distinctive signature. The filename of the image is FTP, which I assume means "Follow the pen." Here's the linked tweet by the President:

Donald J. Trump (from his Twitter account):
If the FBI or DOJ was infiltrating a campaign for the benefit of another campaign, that is a really big deal. Only the release or review of documents that the House Intelligence Committee (also, Senate Judiciary) is asking for can give the conclusive answers. Drain the Swamp!
2:27 PM - 19 May 2018

On the following day, May 20th, Q posted four images showing a street with vehicle and pedestrian traffic at night. Three of the pictures were new. One was a screenshot of a photo he had posted three months earlier, on February 16th, 2018.

May 20 2018 12:40:46 (EST)
NSA_Traf_CAM_ROT1.png
NSA_Traf_CAM_ROT2.png
NSA_Traf_CAM_ROT3.png
DXnq2TRUQAAZUvF.jpg
Note the time.
Note the vehicles on the road.
Compare against 2.16.18.
[6] surv [value targets].
UK:US
US:UK
Q

Q asked anons to note the time and the vehicles on the road and compare the three new images with one he had posted on February 16th. There is a hint that six targets were visible in the photos, that they were under surveillance (surv), and that they were connected to the U.S. and the U.K. governments. Three images have NSA_Traf_CAM in the filename, suggesting that they were obtained from a traffic camera through the NSA's surveillance program. Here is the original information provided by Q with the fourth photo that was first posted on February 16th, 2018:

> Feb 16 2018 20:26:57 (EST)
> NSA_Traf_CAM_LONDON2847.png
> [UK] - Stay Alert.
> Q

In this image, a group of people can be seen crossing a street at night. The location of the scene in all four images was later determined to be near the Corinthia Hotel in London.

An anon commented on the pictures.

> **Anonymous** • May 20 2018
> Q's pics today seem to be a few seconds after the feb pic. In the feb pic they are crossing the street, reaching the median. In today's pic they have crossed the median and have begun crossing the street.
> The two people walking on the sidewalk on the right side of the picture are walking toward the camera.

Q responded, confirming that ROT in the filename indicated "rotation" or a view from the same camera in a different direction.

> May 20 2018 14:04:27 (EST)
> ROT = Rotation.
> Q

I suspected that the photos showed American intelligence agents in London conspiring with British intelligence agents to spy on the Trump campaign. Months later, I compared one person in the photos with a known picture of former FBI attorney Lisa Page. The similarity of their profiles was striking. I posted side-by-side images showing the resemblance of the two people in the photos on Twitter. Q reposted my photos on the research board along with a message to Lisa Page, who evidently, had entered into a plea agreement and was cooperating with investigators.

> Jul 27 2018 10:50:59
> Keep your promise.
> This is not a game.
> Q

Eight minutes later, Q posted again.

> Jul 27 2018 10:58:18 (EST)
> Public awareness forces hand.
> Q

If Lisa Page is a cooperating witness in an investigation of the surveillance of President Trump, public knowledge of her involvement might compel her to abide by her agreement with prosecutors.

Two minutes later, Q posted again.

> Jul 27 2018 11:00:46
> PS round 2.
> [Lead investigator HRC/Russia].
> Q

Apparently, another person shown in the photos was disgraced FBI Special Agent Peter Strzok (PS), who led the bureau's Crossfire Hurricane investigation of President Trump.

On June 11th, 2018, Q asked anons if they had determined the time frame when the London pictures were taken.

> Jun 11 2018
> London pics [prev].
> Year determined?
> Relevant.
> 2015/2016.
> Find the markers [street/surroundings updates]

UK/SIS
WH/C_A/FBI/DOJ
Joint-Treason.
You have a choice.
SIS 'good' agents.
The time is now.
Contact window(s) [GOOD]
Biblical.
Q

Q confirmed my suspicion that the people in the photos were American and British intelligence agents who conspired to spy on President Trump. It seems a window of opportunity had been provided for anyone who wanted to cooperate with investigators.

Regarding the time of year the images were taken and location markers, a famous carousel can be seen in the background of one picture, suggesting a location near Hyde Park. In another photo, the iconic triangular-shaped London Corinthia hotel is visible.

On June 5th, President Trump tweeted about Lisa Page and Peter Strzok and the beginning of the surveillance of his campaign.

Donald J. Trump (from his Twitter account):
Wow, Strzok-Page, the incompetent & corrupt FBI lovers, have texts referring to a counter-intelligence operation into the Trump Campaign dating way back to December, 2015. SPYGATE is in full force! Is the Mainstream Media interested yet? Big stuff!
8:37 PM - Jun 5, 2018

An anon posted a screencap of the President's tweet.

Anonymous • Jun 11 2018
POTUS already told us. Dec 2015.

Then, Q responded with another image showing two people resembling Peter Strzok and Lisa Page at Hyde Park dressed in winter clothing.

Jun 11 2018 12:47:23 (EST)
CLAS_WW_UK_ACTIVE_T.png

Good.
Tweet meant to provide time guide.
What event occurs in Dec (London)?
Think Hyde Park.
Think prev pic [2] people.
Provides Timeframe.
Q

The new photo posted by Q confirmed that FBI attorney Lisa Page and Special Agent Peter Strzok were in London in December 2015. Winter Wonderland is held there each year from mid-November through early January. The FBI claimed it began its counterintelligence investigation of the Trump campaign in July of 2016, but the photos suggest that it began late in 2015.

Now, we'll return to May 20th, 2018, when President Trump posted a tweet demanding that the Department of Justice look into whether the FBI or DOJ infiltrated or spied on his campaign.

Donald J. Trump (from his Twitter account):
I hereby demand, and will do so officially tomorrow, that the Department of Justice look into whether or not the FBI/DOJ infiltrated or surveilled the Trump Campaign for Political Purposes - and if any such demands or requests were made by people within the Obama Administration!
10:37 AM - 20 May 2018

Q posted a screenshot of the tweet along with a few comments.

May 20 2018 12:46:10 (EST)
PAIN.jpg
Follow the PEN.
Think timing.
Coincidence?
The attacks will only get worse.
They are losing [all] control.
Q

Note the file name of the screenshot image in the above post: PAIN. Q gives anons instructions to "follow the pen."

Eight minutes later, Q posted again.

> May 20 2018 12:54:04 (EST)
> Given we have now undeniably [on purpose] verified ourselves to be an inside source, expect the MSM [Clown Army] to attack in full cooperation w/ foreign and domestic assets.
> Be prepared.
> TRUST the plan.
> Conspiracy NO MORE.
> We are in full control.
> PAIN!
> Q

The more evidence Q provides to support the claim that he is close to President Trump, the more the media and rogue intelligence agencies try to silence him. (Q refers to the CIA as Clowns In America.)

The phrase "follow the pen" has multiple meanings. On July 31st, 2018, Q posted another photo of the familiar pen along with a quote from John Adams.

> Jul 31 2018 18:06:03 (EST)
> #1776.png
> "Without the pen of the author of Common Sense, the sword of Washington would have been raised in vain."
> -John Adams
> Q

In this image, the pen is lying on the horizontal axis on a sheet of lined paper. Written on the paper in the foreground is #1776, which matches the image's file name. In the background, something else has been written on the paper, and it is partially visible. It may be the President's signature, but it's difficult to say with certainty since it is partially obscured by the barrel of the pen.

Six months later, Q posted another image of the same pen, but this time, a wristwatch was also present.

> Jan 5 2019 18:19:44 (EST)
> IMG_2616.PNG
> Will POTUS be @ CD tomorrow?

> [1 year delta]
> Matters of NAT SEC?
> The clock is ticking.
> Follow the watch.
> Q

The date of this post was Saturday, January 5th, 2019. The image shows a dark brown folder like the one that holds an Executive Order. The folder is on a desk similar to the one found in the picture a year earlier. The pen rests atop the brown folder, with the watch positioned behind it, showing the time of 3:15. The date is obscured by the minute hand, but the counter shows a single digit that could be a five. An internet search for the image returned no results. As Q noted, this was one day before the one-year anniversary (delta) of the January 6th, 2018 pen post. The President would again be at Camp David (CD) for the weekend. (We will examine this post in more detail in the next chapter).

After Catherine Herridge left Fox News to work for CBS, she began to regularly break news stories on Twitter about the declassification of documents related to the surveillance of the Trump campaign. Herridge typically posts photos of newly declassified documents. Colored highlighters and pens appear in her photos.

An anon wondered if the pens and highlighters were communicating a message.

> **Anonymous** • Jun 5 2020
> Q
> Are Herridge's pen positions comms?

Q replied.

> Follow the pen.
> Have you not been following?
> Q

I've followed Herridge's tweets and observed the pens and highlighters in her posts, but I must confess I do not understand (yet) what message they convey.

CHAPTER 13

Follow the Watch

Q HAS, ON OCCASION, POSTED images of a watch as a way of suggesting that he works with President Trump. In this chapter, we'll examine several of those images. As noted in the previous chapter, on January 5th, 2019, Q posted an image of a pen and a watch.

> Jan 5 2019 18:19:44 (EST)
> IMG_2616.PNG
> Will POTUS be @ CD tomorrow?
> [1 year delta]
> Matters of NAT SEC?
> The clock is ticking.
> Follow the watch.
> Q

The date of this post was Saturday, January 5th, 2019. President Trump was going to be at Camp David (CD) for the weekend. The image shows a dark brown folder like the one that holds an Executive Order. The folder is on a desk. The pen rests atop the folder, with the watch positioned behind it, showing the time of 3:15. The date on the watch may have been the 5th.

The watch appears to be an IWC Portugieser chronograph. There has been no verification yet about who owns it.

Q asked if President Trump was scheduled to be at Camp David the next day (the 6th) and suggested the meeting had to do with matters of national security. Two messages regarding the watch were provided: the clock is ticking, and follow the watch.

On March 2nd, 2019, Q posted an image of the same watch.

> Mar 2 2019 15:54:51 (EST)
> TT.PNG
> The clock is ticking.
> If we are merely a so-called conspiracy (FAKE NEWS NARRATIVE), why the daily attacks by the biggest media co's in the world (attempt to control)?
> You are the news now.
> Q

The time shown on the watch was 3:42. The date shown on the watch was the 2nd. The watch rested in an open notebook with the familiar pen lying beside it. As before, Q wrote, "The clock is ticking."

On March 15th, 2019, Q posted the image he had posted on March 2nd, where the watch showed the time of 3:42.

> Mar 15 2019
> D0ry3OqWwAE1JIZ.jpg
> https://twitter.com/45_Schedule/status/1106643293364985856
> [Marker 1 Complete]
> Q

Q wrote, "Marker 1 Complete," suggesting that the purpose for posting the watch had been fulfilled. Included in this post was a link to a tweet by a Twitter account called POTUS Schedule.

Here is their tweet:

> **POTUS_Schedule** (from their Twitter account):
> Declaration of a National Emergency on the Southern Border

was authorized by US Attorney General William Barr in the Oval Office at 3:42 pm EST.
3:48 PM - 15 Mar 2019

Q reposted the image of the watch that he had posted on January 5th, where time showed 3:15.

Mar 15 2019
Dy7ZYIGUcAQwwS5.jpg
On March 15th?
[3:15]
Q

An anon made a side-by-side graphic displaying the January 5th watch showing the time of 3:15 (the *date* of Attorney General William Barr's announcement) and the watch from March 2nd showing the time of 3:42 (the *time* of Barr's announcement).

Q responded.

Mar 15 2019 15:38:04
The real 'fun' starts soon.
Q

On November 2nd, 2019, after being offline for three months, the Qresearch board returned under a new domain named 8kun. Q posted messages on that board during the month of November but did not interact with anons. He used the same tripcode he had used previously on 8chan, and although tripcodes are secured with a password, many people wanted more proof that this user was, in fact, Q. The following message near the end of November explained that Q would interact with anons once he had a chance to re-verify his identity and prove he was still in control of the tripcode.

Nov 24 2019 19:38:33 (EST)
Future trip(c) re_verify:
Notebook
Pen
Watch

Desk
———————

Anon interaction coming soon.
Q

The following day, Q asked the site administrator, CodeMonkey (CM), if a read-only board could be set up under the name /projectDcomms/. This request by Q would be pending CodeMonkey's approval.

Nov 25 2019 12:33:24 (EST)
New board created [pending approval /CM/]
/projectDcomms/
Q

On December 2nd, 2019, Q posted for the first time on the new board /projectDcomms/. The message indicated that tripcode configuration would commence.

Q !!Hs1Jq13jV6
Dec 2 2019 12:55:59
/trip_config/
Q

Less than a minute later, President Trump tweeted.

Donald J. Trump (from his Twitter account):
The Republican Party has NEVER been so united! This Impeachment Scam is just a continuation of the 3 year Witch Hunt, but it is only bringing us even closer together!
12:56:48 PM - Dec 2, 2019

Eleven minutes later, Q posted again.

Q !!Hs1Jq13jV6
Dec 2 2019 13:07:32
♦♦♦
/trip_confirmed/
/relay_1-99/
Q

Q's post included a graphic showing his previous post alongside the tweet by President Trump. The timestamps showed a 49-second interval. That was the first part of Q's identity re-confirmation. Q's next post was a second confirmation.

Dec 2 2019
IDENconf.PNG
/trip_confirmed2/
/relay_1-99/
Q

The above post included a photograph of the familiar pen and wristwatch. The watch showed the time of 1:29. The date was the 2nd. An internet search for the image returned no results.

Exactly one week later, Department of Justice Inspector General Michael Horowitz's report on the FBI's operation "Crossfire Hurricane" was made public through a link posted on the DOJ Inspector General Twitter account.

The timestamp of the tweet was **1:29 eastern**—the same time shown on the watch image posted by Q a week earlier.

> **Justice OIG** (from their Twitter account):
> DOJ OIG releases Review of Four FISA Applications and Other Aspects of the FBI's Crossfire Hurricane Investigation. View on website here: https://www.justice.gov/storage/120919-examination.pdf View on https://www.oversight.gov/report/doj/review-four-fisa-applications-and-other-aspects-fbi%E2%80%99s-crossfire-hurricane-investigation
> 1:29 pm - 9 Dec 2019

Then-Attorney General William Barr disagreed with some of the findings of the OIG report. His response was posted on the DOJ Twitter account at **1:29 eastern**—the same time shown on the watch image posted by Q.

> **Justice Department** (from their Twitter account):
> Statement by Attorney General William P. Barr on the Inspector General's Report of the Review of Four FISA Applications and Other Aspects of the FBI's Crossfire Hurricane Investigation

https://www.justice.gov/opa/pr/statement-attorney-general-william-p-barr-inspector-generals-report-review-four-fisa
1:29 pm - 9 Dec 2019

U.S. Attorney John Durham likewise disagreed with some of the findings of the report. His response was posted on the Connecticut U.S. Attorney's Twitter account at **1:29 eastern**.

U.S. Attorney CT (from their Twitter account):
Statement of U.S. Attorney John H. Durham
https://go.usa.gov/xpVkk
1:29 pm - 9 Dec 2019

What do you suppose the odds are that these three tweets from the Department of Justice would be posted at the same time, on the same day—*and* at the exact time posted by Q a week earlier? How would Q be aware of this timing? Was Q responsible for the coordination?

CHAPTER 14

Bait Expends Ammunition

Q DISSEMINATES INFORMATION EQUALLY TO his followers and enemies, but has different agendas regarding these two audiences. To friendly followers, he provides information on subjects that must be researched. He also offers encouragement, instruction, clarification, and confirmation. To his enemies, Q supplies information intended to trip them up. It's a tricky proposition, given that friends and enemies are both working with the same information. We were able to observe the interplay between Q and his enemies when a congressional hearing was scheduled for December 5th, 2018, to hear witnesses testify about allegations of corruption related to the William Jefferson Clinton Foundation.

To set the stage, let's look at a post from 2017, where Q suggested that an operation was underway to "capture a very dangerous animal."

Nov 14 2017
How do you capture a very dangerous animal?
Do you attack it from the front?
Do you walk through the front door?
Do you signal ahead of time you will be attacking?
How do you distinguish between good and bad?

Who do you trust to keep secrets?
How do you prevent leaks?
Who do you trust to complete the mission?
How do you prevent warnings being sent?

♦♦♦

Nothing is as it appears.
What show is being put on by AG Sessions since his confirmation?
What show is being put on by POTUS since AG Sessions' confirmation?
Why was AG Sessions' confirmation challenged heavily?
Why was RR's confirmation smooth and easy?
What was the vote count for RR?
Why did Sessions recuse himself?
Why is this relevant?

♦♦♦

What was the DC vote breakdown between Trump & Clinton?
What is the nickname for DC?
Why would sealed indictments be outside of DC jurisdiction?
What purpose would this serve?
Why are judicial appointments being rapidly completed?
Who can you trust?
Have faith, Patriots.
Q

Since Q's stated mission is the disclosure of information pertaining to the removal of corruption, we may infer that the term "dangerous animal" is a euphemism for corrupt people.

As a member of Donald Trump's campaign team, Jeff Sessions met briefly with Russian Ambassador Sergey Kislyak. The press seized on this opportunity and suggested that Sessions had an improper relationship with a Russian dignitary. Sessions acquiesced to pressure and recused himself from the investigation of alleged Russian interference in the 2016 Presidential election. Ever since his recusal, Trump has shown public disdain for Sessions.

Because the Washington D.C. area voted predominantly for Hillary Clinton in 2016, it would be difficult to find unbiased jurors for legal proceedings involving the Clinton Foundation. Q hinted that a federal prosecutor had been appointed in a location less favorable to the Clintons and that indictments were already being sealed at the time of this post.

The above-quoted message from Q was posted on November 14th, 2017, the day after a letter was sent to then-chairman of the House Judiciary Committee, Bob Goodlatte, from Assistant Attorney General Stephen Boyd. Goodlatte had requested a Special Counsel be appointed to investigate allegations of corruption related to the Clinton Foundation. Boyd said the DOJ had appointed "senior federal prosecutors" to evaluate the matters Goodlatte had raised in a previous letter.

In March of 2018, under pressure from members of Congress, Jeff Sessions revealed the name of a prosecutor who was investigating the Clinton Foundation—John Huber, from the Salt Lake City U.S. Attorney's office. The announcement did not thrill many people.

Some thought an investigation by a Special Counsel might be more thorough. Such an investigation would certainly be more public. But the Special Counsel investigation of alleged Russian election interference led by Robert Mueller showed that this process was not foolproof. Rather than proving allegations of collusion with Russia by the Trump campaign, Mueller's team found no evidence of collusion. Instead, they used the investigation to trap Trump's associates in process crimes and claimed that Trump obstructed their investigation, though he was not charged with obstruction.

Mueller's team regularly leaked information to the press, which allowed reporters to create news cycles that damaged the public perception of a President who had done nothing wrong. Watching a Special Counsel investigation being used as a political weapon gave me concern for that process.

The Clinton Foundation investigation took on the exact opposite complexion. Mueller's investigation was the subject of weekly news stories. So far, not one detail had leaked from Huber's investigation to the press. The absence of leaks led some to conclude that Huber's investigation had made no real progress. Some journalists claimed the investigation never began. After all, if Huber was investigating a monstrous nonprofit like the Clinton Foundation, surely some detail would have leaked to the press.

A congressional hearing had been scheduled for December 5th, 2018, to hear testimony about Clinton Foundation corruption. One witness was said to be a whistleblower. The media had reported that U.S. Attorney Huber was also scheduled to testify. The week before the hearing, Q indicated that information had finally been leaked about Huber's investigation. He warned the person responsible for the leak not to say anything more.

Nov 30 2018 21:27:58
To the person who leaked Huber > [Clinton Foundation] Whistleblower' DO NOT reveal more.
MONDAY.
Q

Nineteen minutes later, Q issued another warning.

Nov 30 2018 21:46:11
FIRST AND ONLY LEAK (public) re: HUBER activities.
NO FURTHER DETAILS SHOULD BE RELEASED [WARNING]
PAIN COMING.
Q

An anon posted a transcript of a conversation from Sean Hannity's TV show where investigative journalists John Solomon and Sara Carter discussed a Clinton Foundation whistleblower.

Anonymous • Nov 30 2018 22:26:17
"New Clinton Foundation Whistleblower TBA Next Monday?"

In a discussion between Hannity, John Soloman and Sara Carter, something new came to light about the Clinton Foundation investigation.

HANNITY: Now: there's something percolating that will probably break Monday. You're both smiling. Do either one of you want to give the audience....well, a little heads up.....

JOHN: I'll give you some breaking news right now, Sean. Just two hours ago, federal prosecutors assigned to John Huber, the [Utah] US Attorney investigating the Clintons, reached out to a whistleblower in the Clinton Foundation, [this is the] first time we've seen contact between a Clinton Foundation whistleblower and that particular federal office. That just happened tonight.

HANNITY: Are you talking about the one who's home was raided?

> JOHN S.: No, this is a new—a different whistleblower that you might.....you'll learn a lot on Monday, I betcha.
>
> HANNITY: All right, we'll learn a lot more on Monday. Sara, last word...
>
> SARA: We need to keep our eyes—
>
> HANNITY: What's the preview of Monday's coming attraction?
>
> SARA (big laugh): I think we've got a lot to look forward to on Monday, Sean. And I think the American people are going to see that there was [something] happening behind the scenes at the FBS as well as the Dept of Justice. And Michael Horowitz has been doing a very deep dive into this...There's gonna be a lot of breaking news in the next month and [in] the months to come.
>
> HANNITY: Amazing the year of the boomerang. We were right all along. It continues.
>
> https://www.youtube.com/watch?v=CFhgS8VR58s~20:20

Q responded to the anon.

> Nov 30 2018
> Future will prove past.
> History books.
> JUSTICE.
> Enjoy the show.
> Q

That same day, the death of former President George H.W. Bush was announced. A state funeral was planned for December 5th, the day of the congressional hearing.

Q posted the following message on December 3rd.

> Dec 3 2018 12:42:42
> Odds of a State Funeral on D5?

How many coincidences before mathematically impossible?
♦♦♦
Q

Was it a coincidence that a state funeral was suddenly planned for the same day a congressional hearing was to be held? Q asked about the odds of the funeral falling on D5 (December 5th).

Ten minutes later, Q provided more insights into the purpose of information leaks.

Dec 3 2018 12:52:14
♦♦♦
DOJ [policy] does not discuss ongoing investigations.
Majority of leaks [by them] serve to their benefit.
Some do not.
Some are designed to provide the public w/ a 'glimpse' into the shadows.
Glimpse > Leverage.
Leverage > Panic.
Panic > RATS.
Dark to Light.
Q

Most leaks work in favor of the deep state since they are often used by the media to create stories that support approved political narratives. Some leaks work against them. In this case, the leak about the Clinton Foundation whistleblower caused the bad actors to panic and schedule a funeral in an attempt to prevent (or distract attention away from) a congressional hearing.

Nine minutes later, Q posted again.

Dec 3 2018 13:02:17
The public is about to learn that the DOJ, FBI, + other US/Foreign assets have been actively working behind the scenes in one of the largest criminal investigations in modern day history.
DECLAS > Purpose > illuminate the 'TRUTH' > People

Transparency is the only way forward [CONTROLLED MEDIA - 'Enemy of the People'].

Fourteen minutes later, Q posted again.

> Dec 3 2018 13:16:01
> ♦♦♦
> Postponed.
> Well-played DS.
> Please allow us to counter.
> Q

The congressional hearing on December 5th was postponed until December 13th. Q congratulated the deep state (DS) and hinted that patriots had planned a countermove.

Later that evening, Q posted again.

> Dec 3 2018 21:12:29
> FOX execs pulled (3) scheduled guests.
> Focus: 41
> Q

Q noted that Fox News had cancelled the appearance of three guests that night in order to cover the death of George H.W. Bush, the 41st President.

The next day, Q posted again.

> Dec 4 2018
> ♦♦♦
> "NBC News: There appears, although the redacted documents do not make it completely clear, that there is a [[[+++separate criminal investigation going on outside of Special Counsel Robert Mueller's purview+++]]] for which Flynn has been providing significant assistance."
> Markers are important.
> [Dec 4, 2017] > [Dec 4, 2018]
> Think No Name.
> Did Mueller have a choice in making the recommendation?

Who does Mueller 'now' report to?
Does WHITAKER also oversee HUBER + OIG?
What case(s) is HUBER + OIG + team of 470 currently working on?
Who has the server(s)?
Who has access to NSA UT Term1-12?
Does FISA grant access to NSA umbrella collection?
You are witnessing something [firsthand] that many cannot possibly comprehend or accept as reality [Sci-Fi or precision M_planning?]
Coincidences > > > reveal w/o violating NAT SEC
Coincidences > > > mathematically impossible to be 'FALSE'
Coincidences > > > bypass 'installed' restrictions to prevent future legal attachments
Comms understood? 5:5?
SENATE WAS THE TARGET.
Q

Q quoted NBC News correspondent Tom Winter who reported that General Michael Flynn had been assisting the DOJ in a probe separate from the Mueller investigation. On December 4th, 2017, Q posted, saying that General Flynn was safe. On December 4th, 2018, it was revealed that he was cooperating in a separate criminal investigation, being run by U.S. Attorney John Huber and overseen by then-Acting Attorney General Matt Whitaker. Q pointed out that patriots have access to all information gathered by the NSA and, in particular, anyone under FISA surveillance. The coincidences highlighted reveal information without violating national security laws and they defy mathematical odds. Republican control of the Senate in the 2018 election allowed congressional investigations of corruption to continue.

The following day, December 5th, Q posted again.

Dec 5 2018 00:01:07 (EST)
Logical thinking.
D5 drops 1st - last.
Content & Dates.
Huber drops 1st - last.
Content & Dates.

Role of Huber (as portrayed by 'Q')?
What are the odds (mathematical probability) that Huber would be scheduled to testify re: Clinton Foundation on D5?
What are the odds (mathematical probability) GHWB passes away and the State Funeral date is on D5?
What other interviews and investigations were wiped clean (postponed) given a STATE FUNERAL takes up media coverage for a week?
Why does the (global) FAKE NEWS media [largest in the world] continually attack 'Q'?
Why is the WASH POST leading the attack?
Think ABC agency.
When you are awake you can SEE CLEARLY.
[RAPID_FIRE]
Q

If we examine all the posts by Q that mention D5, we find that they pertain to government abuse of FISA surveillance. U.S. Attorney Huber's role, as portrayed by Q, was to investigate the Clinton Foundation. The odds that Huber would be scheduled to testify on December 5th (D5) and that the hearing would be canceled because of a state funeral are small.

Q pointed out that attacks against him are often led by *The Washington Post*. *The Post* is owned by Jeff Bezos (the former CEO of Amazon), whose organization provided data storage for the CIA via Amazon Web Services at the time of Q's post.

Later that day, an anon posted a photo from the state funeral. President Trump and his wife Melania were in the picture but seemed indifferent to the former presidents who stood next to them.

Anonymous • Dec 5 2018 12:56:46 (EST)
POTUS FLOTUS not participating in this evil.

Q responded.

One man, who gave up everything, risking his life (himself/family), to fight for & defend, We, the PEOPLE.
Bait expends ammunition.
EVIL has no place here.
Q

The statement "bait expends ammunition" suggests that patriots deployed a disinformation campaign to get the deep state to make a wrong move. It has been observed that a state funeral could be held at virtually any time. In a closed casket funeral, the public has no way of verifying the identity of body inside the casket or if there is a body there at all. The announcement that Huber was going to testify before Congress was an attempt to get the deep state to play a valuable card—a move they could only make once. It seems as though the disinformation campaign achieved its objective.

On December 7th, Q posted the following message.

> Dec 7 2018
> ♦♦♦
> Why 'all of a sudden' are people talking about the CLINTON FOUNDATION (including whistleblowers and hidden company established to investigate covertly (ex_ABCs))?
> Would you 'go public' if the investigation was still ongoing?
> What happens when you have enough evidence to PROCEED?
> What is the benefit of educating the public PRIOR TO proceeding?
> COME[Y]
> Q

It was announced that a private firm had been investigating the Clinton Foundation, and its principal investigators were scheduled to testify at the congressional hearing on December 13th. A U.S. Attorney like Huber would not be expected to testify about an ongoing investigation, but a news cycle about his anticipated testimony could be used to raise public awareness and cause bad actors to expend ammunition. This is a tactic used in an information war.

> Dec 12 2018 17:22:57 (EST)
> ♦♦♦
> Schedule for tomorrow.
> Where is HUBER?
> NOBODY IS ABOVE THE LAW.
> THE WORLD IS WATCHING.
> Q

Q noted that U.S. Attorney Huber was not listed as a witness for the Clinton Foundation hearing that would take place the next day.

An anon replied.

> **Anonymous** • Dec 12th 2018
> So HUBER is a HEADFAKE? If so, BRILLIANT Q!

Q responded.

> FALSE.
> HUBER will bring SEVERE PAIN TO DC.
> SESSIONS' forced release of name [HUBER] to House created another variable.
> Use Logic.
> Why would we tell you the plan if in doing so also alerts those who we are actively engaged in HUNTING?
> You are witnessing, first-hand, the demise of those in power [OLD GUARD].
> Those who push simply have no grasp of reality.
> Those who push simply do not understand warfare tactics.
> Emotions cloud judgement.
> Emotions cloud logic.
> You have more than you know.
> Securing the SENATE meant EVERYTHING.
> Securing the SC meant EVERYTHING.
> [Avoided Z]
> We, the PEOPLE.
> ENOUGH IS ENOUGH.
> TOGETHER WE WIN!
> Do you think all these attacks on 'Q' (We, the People) is simply for a person on the internet who they label as a conspiracy?
> Think for yourself.
> Trust yourself.
> Research for yourself.
> Be in control of yourself.
> NEVER let someone else DRIVE YOU.
> Those who try to DRIVE YOU are not your friend.
> Q

Q explained that although Huber's rumored appearance at the hearing was a ploy to get the deep state to make a wrong move, in the end, justice will be delivered.

Many people noticed that envelopes were distributed to former presidents or their wives at the Bush funeral. In some cases, the opening of those envelopes was caught on video and the facial reactions of those who opened the envelopes were noted by the public. Consequently, a lot of emotionally-driven hype and speculation was spread on social media, but Q gave us a simple answer in the exchange below.

An anon asked about the envelopes.

> **Anonymous** • Dec 12 2018
> What were in the envelopes ???

Q replied.

> Our promise to 'counter'.
> Q

On September 24th, 2020, *Fox News* reported that U.S. Attorney Huber's investigation of the Clinton Foundation had been turned over to U.S. Attorney John Durham. We will explore Durham's investigation in the next chapter.

CHAPTER 15
John Durham

DURING THE PRESIDENTIAL ELECTION IN 2016, the Obama FBI surveilled Donald Trump's Presidential campaign through an investigation called "Crossfire Hurricane." General Michael Flynn was surveilled through a parallel investigation named "Crossfire Razor." The FBI's goal was to find (or manufacture) evidence that could be leaked to the press to create a negative public perception of Trump that would prevent him from being elected. After he won the 2016 election, the goal changed. The new objective was sabotaging Trump's first term as President.

The initial tactic employed by the Obama intelligence community was smearing Trump's National Security Adviser, Michael Flynn, in an attempt to remove him from office. Using a series of classified information leaks, the intelligence community and the media created a narrative that Flynn was sympathetic to Russia. Flynn would eventually resign and come under investigation by Robert Mueller, whose far-reaching probe failed to prove that the Trump campaign had colluded with Russia.

The U.S. government's Foreign Intelligence Surveillance Court facilitated the surveillance of the Trump campaign. The FBI and DOJ presented an application to spy on Trump campaign staffer Carter Page, whom they accused of working with a foreign government. The nature of

FISA surveillance allowed the FBI to spy on the entire campaign. Carter Page had been a source for the government; he helped officials with an unrelated investigation. The FBI *knew* this fact but intentionally omitted it when applying for a warrant to surveil him. FBI Attorney Kevin Clinesmith didn't simply *overlook* the information that could have prevented Carter Page from being surveilled; he *altered an email* to reverse the facts entirely and was later prosecuted by U.S. Attorney John Durham. Unfortunately, the damage to Carter Page's reputation was done by the time the details appeared publicly. Finally, in August 2020, Clinesmith pled guilty to falsifying a document to justify the surveillance and became the first co-conspirator charged in the scandal known to many as "Spygate."

On September 16th, 2021, the Department of Justice announced that John Durham had indicted a second Spygate co-conspirator, Michael Sussman, a partner with the law firm Perkins Coie. Sussman pled not guilty to making false statements to the FBI. He provided information to them alleging a connection between Trump and a Russian bank. The media then used that allegation to claim that Trump had illicit ties to a foreign government. The allegation was proven untrue.

The Sussman case brought to light the fact that he was providing information to the FBI on behalf of Trump's political opponent, Hillary Clinton. According to the indictment, Sussman told FBI General Counsel James Baker he was not providing the information on behalf of a client. However, his financial records showed that he was billing his time researching the matter to Hillary Clinton's Presidential campaign, a fact he hid from the bureau. For that, he was charged with making a materially false statement. Sussman was tried but found not guilty by a jury in what former Attorney General Matt Whitaker called a case of jury nullification. Whitaker made the following statement:

> *My biggest concern is the jury foreman came out and really gave up what the jury was discussing, which is that they thought this case should have never been brought to their attention in the first place. And that's a little concerning because this looks more like a jury nullification, where even though the evidence was overwhelming, even though they, the government, proved their case, that the jury just decided that this wasn't a case worth pursuing. So, this case, to me, factually and legally was a slam dunk case. But as I had said earlier, leading up to this jury verdict, this jury was going to be very difficult for Durham and his team to get a conviction.*

Igor Danchenko was next to be charged by John Durham. Danchenko was the primary source of information found in the dossier created by Christopher Steele that was circulated by the press in an attempt to smear Donald Trump. The Steele dossier was also used by the FBI to obtain a warrant to surveil Carter Page, and through him, the 2016 campaign team. The dossier was filled with lies about Trump and his associates. Danchenko was charged with five counts of making materially false statements to the FBI. Durham revealed that Danchenko was put on the FBI payroll as a confidential human source and remained one for three years, despite the fact that he had repeatedly lied to the bureau. In October 2022, Danchenko was found not guilty on all counts.

In May of 2023, John Durham filed a report with the DOJ containing the conclusions of his investigation. He confirmed what many people suspected; that in 2016, the Clinton campaign hatched a plan to accuse then-candidate Trump as having colluded with Russia and the Obama administration put that plan into operation. Durham found that the FBI and DOJ launched their investigation of Trump without a legal predicate. Durham recommended no charges for the Spygate conspirators, saying their deeds amounted to matters of poor judgment, political bias and unprofessionalism, but not criminal behavior

One can hardly blame Durham for not prosecuting the Spygate conspirators. A mountain of evidence had been presented to juries in the Danchenko and Sussman cases, but they were acquitted. It seems unlikely that anyone involved in the surveillance of President Trump would have been convicted.

President Trump has suggested that those who plotted against him committed treason. If so, a civilian court would not be the venue to hear such evidence; the proper venue would be a military court. If Trump returns to the White House, military tribunals may be convened.

On January 23rd, 2023, the U.S. Justice Department announced the arrest of Charles McGonigal, the former Special Agent in Charge of the FBI's New York City counterintelligence division. McGonigal was charged with money laundering and violating U.S. sanctions after working for Russian oligarch Oleg Deripaska. In a separate indictment, McGonigal was charged with receiving $250,000 from Deripaska to investigate a business rival. The arrest is noteworthy in that McGonigal is a close friend of former FBI agent Peter Strzok who led the bureau's Spygate investigation. According to former federal prosecutor Kash Patel, McGonigal played a role in the Spygate investigation. Patel said

McGonigal was responsible for gathering information on Carter page that was used to obtain a warrant to surveil the Trump campaign in 2016 and 2017. In one of his weekly broadcasts, Kash Patel also said that he suspects Durham may have built the case against McGonigal and then handed it off to the U.S. Attorney in New York.

Before leaving the White House, Barack Obama signed an order that increased sharing of intelligence among government agencies. This created an increased visibility to sensitive matters that were leaked by intelligence agencies to the press. After taking office in January 2017, President Trump made it clear to then-Attorney General Jeff Sessions that he expected the intelligence leaks to stop, and those responsible for them to be held accountable. In a public news conference on August 4th, 2017, Sessions made the following statement:

> *While the Department of Justice does not discuss ongoing investigations or confirm specific matters, it is important for the American people—and for those who might be thinking about leaking sensitive or classified information—to know that criminals who would illegally use their access to our most sensitive information to endanger our national security are, in fact, being investigated and prosecuted. Since January, the Department has more than tripled the number of active leak investigations compared to the number pending at the end of the last Administration. And we have already charged four people with unlawfully disclosing classified material or with concealing contacts with foreign intelligence officers.*

Sessions went on to say that U.S. Attorneys had been instructed to prioritize leak investigations, though he did not name the prosecutors he had assigned to this task.

On July 24th, 2020, the *Washington Examiner* published an article revealing that U.S. Attorney John Durham was investigating leaks of classified information to the media regarding General Mike Flynn.

On December 12th, 2018, the day before U.S. Attorney John Huber was supposed to testify before Congress regarding an investigation into the Clinton Foundation, Q posted the following message, which we looked at in the last chapter.

Dec 12 2018 17:22:57 (EST)
♦♦♦
Schedule for tomorrow.

> Where is HUBER?
> NOBODY IS ABOVE THE LAW.
> THE WORLD IS WATCHING.
> Q

Q then responded to this post, suggesting that another prosecutor had been assigned to investigate institutional corruption.

> Dec 12 2018 17:33:56 (EST)
> What if there's another prosecutor (outside of DC) assigned by SESSIONS w/ the same mandate/authority?
> ONE FOR THE HISTORY BOOKS?
> NOT LONG NOW.
> Q

This was the first allusion to U.S. Attorney Durham by Q, though his name was not mentioned. Q first mentioned Durham by name seven months later, in July of 2019.

> Jul 9 2019
> AG & Rogers meeting?
> Durham & Rogers meeting(s)?
> Why did Rogers retire?
> Why did Rogers visit POTUS @ TT w/o authorization shortly after a SCIF was installed?
> Why did select former ABC directors call for the removal of Rogers?
> Why did POTUS move his transition command center (base of ops) from TT the VERY NEXT DAY?
> Q

Those who have closely followed the Spygate scandal know that former NSA director Admiral Mike Rogers met with President Trump's transition team after a SCIF had been installed in Trump tower (TT). SCIF stands for Sensitive Compartmented Information Facility. It's a device used to prevent eavesdropping when sensitive information is shared. Evidently, Rogers provided a classified briefing about the surveillance of the campaign. He met Trump's team without authorization from his superiors, which caused them to demand that he be fired. The day after meeting with Rogers, Trump moved the transition team headquarters to his resort in Bedminster, New Jersey. What we didn't know was that apparently, Admiral Rogers also met with Durham.

On September 24th, 2019, the text messages of former FBI employees were made public as part of a federal court filing in Michael Flynn's case. In one text from April 11th, 2017, FBI attorney Lisa Page discussed the first time she met with U.S. Attorney Durham. In the same text message, she said FBI General Counsel James Baker called her into his office to discuss the meeting. If Page met with Durham over her involvement in the surveillance of Trump, that puts the beginning of Durham's investigation at a time prior to mid-April of 2017. After the text messages were released, *Fox News* published a story reporting that U.S. Attorney Durham had assumed control of the Clinton Foundation investigation from U.S. Attorney John Huber.

Q responded to the news.

> Sep 26 2020
> What did we learn this week?
> 1. Durham 'true' start?
> 2. Durham 'take-over' Huber [select parts re: CF-i]?
> What if there's another prosecutor (outside of DC) assigned by SESSIONS w/ the same mandate/authority?
> Q

On October 5th, 2017, while meeting with the families of military leaders, President Trump made a statement to the press who were in attendance. He said, "Do you know what this represents? Maybe it's the calm before the storm." A perplexed reporter asked, "What storm, Mister President?" In an ominous tone, Trump replied, "You'll find out."

On November 11th, 2019, Q tied several dates together.

> Nov 11 2019 18:23:51 (EST)
> "Calm Before the Storm." - POTUS
> Month/Day 'Q' public campaign initiated?
> Month/Day 'Durham' initiated?
> What famous crime family did Durham target?
> "Also spearheaded mob prosecutions of the [Gambino],

Genovese and Patriarca crime families."
http://content.time.com/time/nation/article/0,8599,1918738,00.html
What AB[C] agency did Durham target?
How are messages sent?
https://www.rollingstone.com/culture/culture-news/frank-cali-murder-mafia-boss-qanon-motive-anthony-comello-861777/
[Dec 12 2018]
"What if there's another prosecutor (outside of DC) assigned by SESSIONS w/ the same mandate/authority?" - Q
Do you believe in coincidences?
5:5?
Be ready, Patriots.
Q

Although he served as an interim U.S. Attorney during 2017, John Durham was sworn in as U.S. Attorney for Connecticut on October 28th, 2017, which happens to be the same day Q first posted. During his career, Durham has investigated a number of organized crime figures, including James "Whitey" Bulger, Stephen "The Rifleman" Flemmi, and the Gambino, Genovese, and Patriarca crime families. He has also investigated corrupt FBI agents and was tapped by then-Attorney General Eric Holder to investigate allegations of abuse by the CIA in its use of torture against terror suspects.

On December 14th, 2019, Q suggested that the beginning of his public information operation, and Durham's start as U.S. Attorney for Connecticut on the same day, was not a coincidence.

Dec 14 2019
Month/day 'Durham' initiated?
Month/day 'Q' public campaign initiated?
How many coincidences before mathematically impossible?
It was over before it began.
Q

In January of 2020, Q pointed out that declassification and release of certain documents might be precluded by grand jury investigations, since information released to the public might bias potential jurors.

Jan 23 2020
DECLAS CoC
POTUS > Barr
Barr > Durham
[[F] classified intel provided [FVEY - Non FVEY] as needed]
Does Durham want to hold [freeze] 'public' declas due to criminal nature of the probe(s)?
Think GJ material.
When did the investigation begin?
When did the investigation really begin?
Nothing can stop what is coming.
Nothing.
Slow drip > Flood
Q

The chain of command (CoC) for declassification begins at the top with the President. Donald Trump had authorized then-Attorney General William Barr to declassify documents related to Spygate. Since it is apparent that Durham is the lead prosecutor, any documents to be declassified would need to be cleared through him, as he would know which ones could be presented to grand juries. Q asked if it logically followed that Durham might block the declassification and release of any documents pertaining to his investigation. He then asked when Durham's investigation is believed to have started and when it actually started. As I pointed out earlier, it seems Lisa Page first met with Durham regarding her involvement in Spygate prior to her text about that meeting on April 11, 2017. That would put the start of Durham's investigation several years *before* the publicly-acknowledged time frame.

The first image posted by Q was on October 31, 2017. It was the famous painting of George Washington crossing the Delaware River to Trenton, New Jersey, on Christmas night in 1776. The filename chosen for the image was Patriots.jpg. The post was about military intelligence. Here's the text of the post:

Oct 31 2017 22:00:15 (EST)
Patriots.jpg
SCI[F]
Military Intelligence.
What is 'State Secrets' and how upheld in the SC?

What must be completed to engage MI over other (3) letter agencies?
What must occur to allow for civilian trials?
Why is this relevant?
What was Flynn's background?
Why is this relevant?
Why did Adm R (NSA) meet Trump privately w/o auth?
Does POTUS know where the bodies are buried?
Does POTUS have the goods on most bad actors?
Was TRUMP asked to run for President?
Why?
By Who?
Was HRC next in line?
Was the election suppose to be rigged?
Did good people prevent the rigging?
Why did POTUS form a panel to investigate?
Has POTUS *ever* made a statement that did not become proven as true/fact?
What is POTUS in control of?
What is the one organization left that isn't corrupt?
Why does the military play such a vital role?
Why is POTUS surrounded by highly respected generals?
Who guards former Presidents?
Why is that relevant?
Who guards HRC?
Why is ANTIFA allowed to operate?
Why hasn't the MB been classified as a terrorist org?
What happens if Soros funded operations get violent and engage in domestic terrorism?
What happens if mayors/ police comms/chiefs do not enforce the law?
What authority does POTUS have specifically over the Marines?
Why is this important?
What is Mueller's background? Military?
Was Trump asked to run for President w/ assurances made to prevent tampering?
How is POTUS always 5-steps ahead?
Who is helping POTUS?

One line in the post has a typo that was never corrected by Q:

Was the election suppose to be rigged?

The word "supposed" is missing the letter "d." Typos are usually corrected unless they're intentional. Was there a secret meaning behind this typo?

An anon posted an interesting fact he had uncovered about the boat used by Washington to cross the Delaware River. This particular type of vessel is called a "Durham" boat.

Q responded to the discovery.

> Jan 28 2020 14:46:22 (EST)
> DurhamBoat.jpg
> https://en.wikipedia.org/wiki/Durham_boat
> Anons found the subtle hint dropped in the beginning.
> Think Durham start.
> Think 'Q' start.
> You have more than you know.
> Q

The name of the boat used by Washington begins with the letter "d," the same letter that was missing from the word "supposed" in this post. Coincidentally, the boat has the same name as a federal prosecutor who was sworn in the day Q's operation began. President Trump happened to be holding a rally in Trenton, New Jersey, the night this discovery was made. Trenton was the city where Washington's troops landed after crossing the Delaware.

> Jan 28 2020 15:20:07 (EST)
> https://twitter.com/elenochle/status/1210799795075350533
> Do you believe in coincidences?
> Where is the rally held tonight?
> Enjoy the show!
> Q

CHAPTER 16

Trust the Plan

Q HAS ASSERTED THAT A plan is in place to remove institutional corruption around the globe. When followers become worried or discouraged, Q sometimes tells them, "Trust the plan."

When I was a boy, I had fears that could be considered common to most children. I told my father about them, and his response usually set my mind at ease. He didn't tell me the world was perfect. He never promised that I would avoid pain or loss. My fears were irrational. The odds that they would happen were small, and my father knew that. He had a perspective that I didn't. He presented his views in a way that I could grasp. Few of my fears ever came to pass. My father was proven right, and over time, his tendency to be right caused me to trust his judgment. That same principle applies to us. Because we lack firsthand knowledge of the events Q discusses, we are asked to trust him and President Trump. Allow me to share a practical application of that principle.

President Trump battled Congress for two years over funding for a wall on the southern U.S. border. Many people believed it would never be built because Congress opposed the wall construction. They feared that Trump would lose his battle with Congress and assumed there was no other plan. But a handful of anons had a different perspective.

In March of 2018, Q posted the following message:

```
Mar 23 2018
Clock activated.
RED_CASTLE.
GREEN_CASTLE.
Stage_5:5[y]
Q
```

Anons who researched this post uncovered the fact that the Army Corps of Engineers has a red castle on its insignia, and a branch of the Corps is located in Greencastle, Indiana. We concluded that this post was a hint that the Army Corps of Engineers would build the wall on the southern border, and the Defense Department would fund it. Nine months later, our theory was proven right when the President formally announced his plan to have the military build and fund the wall.

President Trump never intended to obtain funding for the wall from Congress. His open battle with Congressional leaders was to expose their desire to keep the southern border open to facilitate drug, weapons, and human trafficking. Trump planned all along to fund the wall using the Defense Department budget, which anons knew about nine months before it was made public. The President had a plan. Q revealed it to anons.

When Q asks us to trust the plan, it's usually in reference to a specific subject we're concerned about but over which the President has control. Q merely points out that they have a different perspective on that issue. They have greater knowledge. They know the eventual outcome and don't want us to worry about it.

When a message by Q goes viral in the anon community, it becomes a target for critics. The phrase "trust the plan" has been broadly criticized by social media influencers. Those who are hostile to Q claim that "trust the plan" is an order to stand down, disengage and do nothing while tyrants destroy our country. Q detractors have created a false dichotomy: you can either trust the plan or you can fight tyranny yourself, but you cannot do both.

Q uses the exhortation "trust the plan" only when certain issues are raised. For example, when matters of foreign policy or national security are discussed, Q might tell us to trust the plan. It's the most appropriate response when an operational plan is in place to deal with an issue that is beyond the control of average citizens. On the other hand, when the issue involves Marxist indoctrination in public schools, Q might tell us to get involved and make our voices heard.

Q's goal is to provide average citizens with information and motivate them to take back power from corrupt leaders and institutions.

> Mar 3 2018
> Stay TOGETHER.
> Be STRONG.
> Get ORGANIZED.
> Be HEARD.
> FIGHT the censorship.
> You, the PEOPLE, have ALL the POWER.
> You simply forgot how to PLAY.
> TOGETHER you are INVINCIBLE.
> They want you divided.
> They want you silenced.
> MAKE NOISE.
> We are WITH you.
> MAKE IT RAIN.
> Q

We must make a distinction between trusting the plan and knowing the *details* of the plan. When we assume we know the plan's details, we're tempted to predict how future events will play out. After anons had made a series of failed predictions about how events would unfold in April 2020, Q posted a caution about making predictions.

> Apr 10 2020
> Patriots: be cautious in your interpretations of info posted.
> False expectations [& push] based on 'speculation' will only weaponize those who attack us [MSM].
> Why does [MSM] expend resources [daily] attempting to discredit?
> Do you provide the playbook to the enemy w: specific dates?
> Logical thinking.

♦♦♦

Many people have had their hopes dashed by failed predictions about Q's messages. Some of the blame lies with us. We are responsible for managing our expectations. Some fault rests on decoders who failed to recognize that Q did not intend predictions to be made and disseminated. He intended the exact opposite. He told anons to wait for big news to drop, and when it does, review his posts (the graphic) for clues about the latest news story. This approach would help confirm Q's foreknowledge.

> Nov 4 2017
> When big news drops please re-read entire graphic.
> This is so critical and why information is provided in a certain order and why some topics are continually emphasized more than others as those will be the recent happenings.
> This is the purpose of this new thread (re-organize).
> Snow White
> Wizards & Warlocks.
> Q

Predictions about future events can only be made if one thinks they understand the details of the plan. Q never reveals the details of a plan overtly. If they were given to us, they would be revealed to Q's enemies. If an enemy knew the details of a plan, that plan could not be carried out without risk to operators, and it would have to be scrapped. Q asks us to trust the plan because its details cannot be disclosed for reasons of operational security.

Covid-19 and the Election

Many people interpreted Q's drops as a guarantee that Donald Trump would win the 2020 election. However, Trump and Q had been warning of the effort to steal the election through mail-in voting.

In March of 2020 professional sports organizations in the U.S. announced new attendance policies related to the Covid-19 pandemic. Before long, nearly all spectator sporting events were held without audiences over fear that in-person attendance would worsen the pandemic. Many businesses closed due to pandemic measures. Some would never reopen. Several states announced their intent to mail out ballots to voters for the November general election. The move was justified by claiming that in-person voting would worsen the pandemic. California Governor Newsom said he would send a ballot to every voter in the state, a move that Hillary Clinton applauded.

Hillary Clinton (from her Twitter account)
I hope other governors around the country follow @GavinNewsom's lead. No voter should be forced to choose between their safety and exercising their civic duty this fall.
2:22 PM - 8 May, 2020

President Trump saw the pandemic as an opportunity for corrupt people to steal the November election through vote-by-mail and tweeted his numerous concerns.

Donald J. Trump (From his Twitter account)
There is NO WAY (ZERO!) that Mail-in Ballots will be anything less than substantially fraudulent. Mail boxes will be robbed, ballots will be forged & even illegally printed out & fraudulently signed. The Governor of California is sending Ballots to millions of people, anyone.....
8:17 AM - 26 May, 2020

....living in the state, no matter who they are or how they got there, will get one. That will be followed up with professionals telling all of these people, many of whom have never even thought of voting before, how, and for whom, to vote. This will be a Rigged Election. No way!
8:17 AM - 26 May, 2020

House Speaker Nancy Pelosi posted this tweet.

Nancy Pelosi (from her Twitter account)
Voting at home shouldn't be a question of politics. It's a health issue. No American should have to choose between their protecting their health and exercising their right to vote. #inners
6:19 AM - 27 May, 2020

Q responded to Pelosi's tweet.

May 27 2020 10:52:06
https://twitter.com/SpeakerPelosi/status/1265633731068518407

> Was this ever about the health and well-being of people?
> Was this ever about the virus?
> Or, was this ALWAYS ABOUT THE ELECTION?
> Q

Seven months before the vote, Q and President Trump warned that corrupt political operators intended to steal the election. Trump had done too much damage to their established system, and they would remove him from power one way or another. He did his best to run a winning campaign. His rallies drew tens of thousands of people. Joe Biden didn't bother to campaign much in public. In-person attendance at his public appearances was discouraged under the cover of the pandemic. Trump's official vote total was 12 million more than he'd received in 2016. Nevertheless, Joe Biden was declared the winner of the 2020 election.

For several months, Trump supporters held out hope that the counting of the Electoral College votes on January 6th, 2021, might provide an opportunity to make things right. Trump's enemies in Congress realized what had been planned for that day, and a riot broke out at the Capitol that ended any attempt to challenge the electoral count. On January 20th, Joe Biden was inaugurated. Millions of patriots spent the next few months searching for answers—looking for any shred of hope.

In 2021, the Arizona State Senate audited the 2020 election in Maricopa County. The audit examined more than 2 million ballots, as well as voting machines and electronic data. One finding that came to light was the fact that on February 2nd, 2021, the day before Maricopa County's auditors began their own limited audit, the entire election database was deleted from the election management system. Multiple problems arose in the 2022 election which will be covered in a future volume in this series.

The audit in Arizona was visited by legislators from 19 other states. Pennsylvania, Texas, and Wisconsin also began audits, while lawsuits were filed in Georgia and Michigan to gain access to ballots from the November 2020 election. Despite claims by politicians and the media that there was no evidence of fraud in the election, 18 states disagreed and enacted new laws aimed at decreasing election fraud by July 14th, 2021.

Consequences of the Biden Presidency

One of President Joe Biden's first moves after being inaugurated was shutting down the Keystone XL pipeline, which led to the loss of American energy independence. The Defense Department under Donald Trump had put together a plan to withdraw from the war in Afghanistan that would prevent the Taliban from assuming control of the country. According to Kash Patel, who served as Chief of Staff to Acting Secretary of Defense Chris Miller, Biden's people were not interested in being briefed on the withdrawal plan. Under Biden's orders, the U.S. military withdrew completely from Afghanistan, leaving more than $80 billion worth of military equipment behind along with hundreds of U.S. citizens. A drone strike that was said to have targeted an ISIS terrorist turned out to have killed an innocent aid worker and his family. Biden claimed he had not been advised by anyone to leave U.S. troops in country. However, when they testified under oath to Congress, CENTCOM Commander General Kenneth McKenzie and Chairman of the Joint Chiefs of Staff General Mark Milley both said they advised Biden to leave 2,500 troops in Afghanistan, or it would immediately fall to the Taliban. Biden ignored their advice, and within hours, the Taliban assumed control from the Afghan government.

Biden reversed many of Donald Trump's immigration policies, would not allow the southern border wall to be finished, and went as far as to ignore a Supreme Court ruling requiring the reinstatement of Trump's "remain in Mexico" policy. All of this has caused a crisis at the southern border. Inflation is the highest it has been in decades. North Korea is testing ballistic missiles for the first time in years. Iran is threatening to enrich uranium to weapons grade.

Joe Biden has proven to be a failure as President. Only a few months into his first term, many who despised Trump found themselves wishing he was back in the White House. Some of us had to see for ourselves what life would be like if Trump lost the election. And that begs the question of whether Trump knew he would lose the election and if he developed a plan with that fact in mind.

CHAPTER 17

Nothing Can Stop What Is Coming

MANY TRUMP SUPPORTERS LOST HOPE that a remedy to their election woes would materialize. Q posted the following message nine days after the 2020 Presidential election.

> Nov 12 2020
> Shall we play a game?
> [N]othing [C]an [S]top [W]hat [I]s [C]oming
> NCSWIC
> https://www.cisa.gov/safecom/NCSWIC
> Who stepped down today [forced]?
> https://www.cisa.gov/bryan-s-ware
> More coming?
> Why is this relevant?
> How do you 'show' the public the truth?
> How do you 'safeguard' US elections post-POTUS?
> How do you 'remove' foreign interference and corruption and install US-owned voter ID law(s) and other safeguards?
> It had to be this way.

> Sometimes you must walk through the darkness before you see the light.
>
> Q

Q often tells us, "Nothing can stop what is coming." What is coming is the exposure of corruption and the prosecution of its perpetrators. In this post, NCSWIC is used as an acronym for this statement, but also for the National Council of Statewide Interoperability Coordinators. According to the linked website, the Council was established by the Department of Homeland Security's Cybersecurity and Infrastructure Security Agency (CISA) in July 2010 to support "Statewide Interoperability Coordinators (SWIC) from the 56 states and territories, by developing products and services to assist them with leveraging their relationships, professional knowledge, and experience with public safety partners involved in interoperable communications at all levels of government."

Elections are considered critical infrastructure in the United States. As such, their security comes under the oversight of CISA. The second link in the above post is to the webpage for CISA's Assistant Director for Cybersecurity, Brian Ware, whom Q suggested was forced to resign after the election. Q hinted that more terminations were coming. He then asked how the public could be shown the truth about corrupt elections and how elections could be safeguarded in the future. Hundreds of new election laws would never have been enacted were it not for problems found in the 2020 election.

It's possible that there was no practical way to prevent the election from being stolen. If that were true, the best plan would be to catch the thieves in the act and present the evidence to the public after the crime had been committed. The downside of such a plan is that Trump would lose the election. The upside is that the public would learn the truth about our elections. As painful as it has been to watch, it seems that allowing corrupt people to brazenly steal an election was the only way to prevent it from happening in the future.

This is not to say that elections will immediately become trustworthy. As long as a majority of citizens believe that elections can be trusted, the problems will remain. The 2022 midterm elections in the U.S. showed little change. The 2022 election in Maricopa County, Arizona, was marred with scandal. Although it is frustrating to watch multiple election cycles repeat the same problems, the public is becoming more convinced that elections are not fair. A May 2023 Rasmussen poll showed that

62 percent of U.S. voters from all parties believe that cheating affected the outcome of the 2020 Presidential election. When a critical mass of voters become convinced that the election system is corrupt, they have a more compelling reason to force state and local governments to make the needed changes.

It would not have occurred to most of us that stolen elections might be part of a larger plan to save our nation and the world. That isn't the way we would do it. And that is the difference between knowing the details of a plan and trusting the plan. Trusting a plan requires us to admit that our understanding is inadequate. It asks us to trust that the knowledge and expertise of another are superior and that they're sufficient to address the situation at hand. It's tempting to assess our odds of victory by looking at the present situation. But those who are working on our behalf are working from a plan that spans many years. It is unrealistic to expect immediate changes to be made to a corrupt system that has been around for hundreds (perhaps thousands) of years. Changing the system will not happen until a critical mass of humanity has been awakened to the reality of institutional corruption. We can take heart in knowing that each year, more people are coming out of their slumber.

I am often asked to speculate about the future of mankind. As of this writing, there is no consensus among Q researchers about the future of America or the world. Some are convinced that the plan failed and the deep state remains in control. It's not difficult to understand why some embrace this view. None of the major players on the global stage have been held accountable. Elections are still being stolen. And we're facing the possibility of World War III. If you take things at face value, it's a dismal picture.

Others take the view that patriots are literally in full control of the major events playing out on the world stage. These researchers believe most of the people who appear to be working *against* President Trump and Q are secretly working *with* them. Most of what looks like hostility toward Trump is said to be political theater. They believe that at a future time, the tide will turn and justice will prevail and some who appeared to be the enemies of Trump will be revealed as secret allies.

I think the truth is somewhere in the middle. I suspect that some aspects of the plan did not go as anticipated, but that is to be expected. Any battle plan only remains intact until first contact with an enemy. Once an enemy is engaged, the plan's effectiveness must be assessed and it must be modified accordingly.

Some have suggested that Donald Trump intended to lose the 2020 election because doing so would create a situation where corruption could be publicly exposed. It is difficult for me to believe that Trump intended to lose the election to prove a point. While he certainly understood the odds that the election might be stolen, I don't think his goal was to lose.

Notwithstanding, the results of the 2020 election set into motion events that are exposing corruption and incompetence in the highest levels of government. For example, as this book goes to print, members of Congress have demanded from the FBI a copy of a specific document reported by a whistleblower to show proof that the Biden family accepted bribes from a foreign government. U.S. Attorney David Weiss has been investigating the financial transactions of Joe Biden's son, Hunter. That investigation could uncover evidence of crimes committed by other members of the Biden family. The DOJ appointed Special Prosecutors to investigate Donald Trump and Joe Biden for possessing classified documents. As President, Donald Trump had the right to declassify any document. The documents possessed by Biden were retained prior to his time in the White House. Possession of them constitutes a violation of federal law.

While Joe Biden's time in the White House has certainly provided an opportunity for the exposure of criminal activity, I suspect that these issues could be exposed in a different way on a different timeline. I believe Trump intended to win the 2020 election so he could battle the deep state from a position of power. However, having been declared the loser, he is being forced to work a different plan from outside the White House.

It seems some of us may have had unrealistic expectations about how long it would take to remove systemic corruption. But despite the apparent lack of results to date, I am optimistic that given enough time, patriots will be victorious. Too many people have been awakened to the realities of corruption and they are not going back to sleep. Those who are awake will continue to spread the truth to those who are taking the sleeping pill.

Jan 27 2018
Chatter exploding.
Change of narrative will be required.
[-4][-5]
Public to awaken [mass-start].
Sleeping pill reject.
OP Mockingbird FAILURE.
FAKE>REAL.

BLIND>20/20.
KILL_CHAIN.
Where we go one, we go ALL>
Q

The plan may have changed, but I'm still trusting it. In time, the truth will be exposed and criminals in positions of power will be held accountable. Trusting the plan is not an exercise of blind faith. Blind faith is trust without knowledge. Q has given us knowledge that seemed impossible for some of us to grasp ten years ago. Trusting the plan is realizing that good people have been contending with evil, and they're still in the fight. Even when it seems like evil has won, if one waits, information becomes available that suggests the battle is not over. The ability of good people to continue the fight has earned them a degree of trust.

May 13 2018
Trust must be earned.
Trust is not blind, nor is truth.
We fight every sigle day on behalf of you, the people who put us here.
We knew this day would come.
We will never forget.
Do not glorify us.
We are merely the vehicle.
You are what matters.
You are hope.
You are love.
You are peace.
Stay united.
Stay together.
Stay strong.
This is bigger than any one person or entity.
You are fighting for truth - collectively.
Will of the people.
Trust in yourself.
The choice will always be yours.
God bless you all.
Where we go one, we go ALL.
Q+

ABOUT THIS SERIES

Q Chronicles is a series that explores the topics and signatures of Q as well as news relevant to the "Great Awakening."

ABOUT THE AUTHOR

Dave Hayes is a teacher, public speaker, and author. He has written more than a dozen books on faith and the spiritual life under the pen name Praying Medic.

GLOSSARY

Because Q's posts include terms you may not be familiar with, I've provided a glossary to help decode abbreviations, acronyms, symbols, names, and agencies. The decodes I've provided are not to be taken as the only possible correct ones. There are, no doubt, valid decodes I have not considered and have not included. Some abbreviations have been confirmed by Q to have multiple meanings. As Q's mission continues, some abbreviations that have been used in one way may later be used in a different way. In such cases, the context of a particular post should be used to determine the best interpretation. The terms in this glossary are not exclusive to posts found in this book. They pertain to the entirety of Q's operation to date.

Note: names and initials are alphabetized as they appear in Q posts which is usually the first name followed by the last name.

/calmbeforethestorm/ or **/CBTS/** — An 8chan board where Q has posted.

/greatawakening/ or **/GA/** — A read-only board on 8chan where Q has posted.

/patriotsfight/ or **/pf/** — An 8chan board where Q has posted messages.

/pb — Previous Bread. A term indicating that a current post refers to a message found in a previous thread (or in the vernacular of anons, a previous bread).

/pol/ — Boards on 4chan and 8chan where Q has posted messages.

/projectdcomms/ — A read-only board on 8kun where Q posts.

/qresearch/ — Boards on 8chan and 8kun where anons can interact with Q.

/thestorm/ — An 8chan board where Q has posted messages.

/_ — A three-sided shape used by Q to illustrate the power structure of the three wealthiest and most politically influential families in the world; the Saudi royal family (removed from power in 2017) the Rothschilds, and George Soros. Q's mission involves the gradual removal of all three sides of the triangle, representing the removal of these families from power.

@jack — Jack Dorsey, who is the CEO of Twitter, a social media platform, and the CEO of Square, a mobile payment processing company.

#2 — Andrew McCabe, Deputy Director of the FBI from February 2016 to January 2018. Later, McCabe became Acting Director of the FBI briefly—May 9th to August 2nd, 2017—after Director James Comey was fired, but McCabe then returned to his Deputy Director position until he was fired by Jeff Sessions in March of 2018.

#FLY# — Q uses the word FLY along with a name and pound sign (#) to indicate a person whose influence has been neutralized or a politician who has been removed from office.

#FlyALFly# — Signified the resignation of Congressman Al Franken.

#FlyCoatsFly# — Signified the removal of Dan Coats as President Trump's Director of National Intelligence.

#FLYJOHNNYFLY — Signified the resignation of John Conyers from the United States Congress.

Glossary

##FLYMAYFLY## — Signified the announcement by Teresa May that she would step down as the Conservative party leader and Prime Minister of the UK.

#FLYROTHFLY# — Signified the reduction of political influence by the Rothschild family.

#FLYSIDFLY# — Two possibilities. This may have signified the end of Arizona Senator John Sidney McCain's time as a U.S. Senator, or it may signify the removal of the influence of Sidney Blumenthal, a trusted associate of Hillary Clinton.

#FLY[RR]FLY# — Signified the resignation of Rod Rosenstein as U.S. Deputy Attorney General.

[] — Brackets indicate different things depending on the context. Q answered an anon's inquiry by indicating that brackets signified a "kill box" but sometimes brackets are used to highlight letters that spell out a message hidden within a post, for example, [p], [r], [a], [y]. Brackets can also be used to disrupt computer programs used by opponents that search Q's posts for key words.

[30] — A time interval, typically 30 days or one month. In some cases, it will signify 31 or 28 days, depending on the number of days in the month.

[93   dk] — 93 dark seems to be a prediction of the 93 days between August 1st and November 2nd of 2019 that Q would not post after 8chan went offline and before its replacement, 8kun, went live.

[C] — Multiple meanings. Often used to indicate the CIA in the term AB[C]. Occasionally, it signifies former Director of National Intelligence Dan Coats or former FBI Director James Comey. It has also been used to signify COVID. In one instance, it refers to classified documents, and in another it appears to indicate the Ted Cruz's 2016 Presidential campaign.

[D] — Two possible decodes. Often used to signify members of the Democratic party. Sometimes signifies declassification of documents.

[E] — Gate E at Terminal 2 in Shanghai Pudong International Airport (PVG).

[F] — Foreign

The Q Chronicles • Book 3: This Is Not a Game

[R] — Several meanings. Used once to refer to the Republican party, and once to refer to the name Rothschild. Used multiple times to indicate Barack Obama, whose Secret Service code name was "Renegade." Obama was referred to by the single letter R in text messages between former FBI employees Lisa Page and Peter Strzok.

[T2] — Terminal 2 at Shanghai Pudong International Airport (PVG).

(6+) — George Soros, a hedge fund billionaire who is known for using his wealth to fund his own brand of political activism. Recipients of his philanthropy appreciate his money, but those who oppose his political views see him as a creator of chaos around the world, and a destabilizing force on economies and societies. Some countries have either banned Soros or restricted his organizations from operating within their borders. These countries include Pakistan, Poland, Turkey, Russia, Soros' home country of Hungary, and the Philippines. The Israeli government has said Soros is not welcome there.

(6++) — The Rothschilds, an influential banking family that exerted economic and political influence over Europe during the 18th and 19th centuries and over the world during the 20th and 21st centuries.

(6+++) — Saudi Arabia, a nation ruled by a hereditary monarchy—the House of Saud. The king serves as head of state and the head of the government.

(You) — When viewing posts on 4chan, 8chan, or 8kun, the word "you" is displayed in parenthesis to indicate that you are viewing your own post.

+ — George Soros, a hedge fund billionaire who is known for using his wealth to fund his own brand of political activism. Recipients of his philanthropy appreciate his money, but those who oppose his political views see him as a creator of chaos around the world—a destabilizing force on economies and societies. Some countries have either banned Soros or restricted his organizations. These countries include Pakistan, Poland, Turkey, Russia, Soros' home country of Hungary, and the Philippines. The Israeli government has said Soros is not welcome there.

++ — The Rothschilds, an influential banking family that exerted economic and political influence over Europe during the 18th and 19th centuries and over the world during the 20th and 21st centuries.

Glossary

+++ — Saudi Arabia, a nation ruled by a hereditary monarchy—the House of Saud. The king serves as head of state and the head of the government.

+++Adm R+++ — Retired Admiral Mike Rogers, former Director of the NSA.

*** — Three asterisks, or three stars, signifying retired Lieutenant General Michael Flynn. In the U.S. Army and some other branches of the military, a lieutenant general is a three-star general officer.

0 Delta — A term signifying posts by Q and President Trump at the same time.

1+1 = 2 or 2 + 2 = 4 — When the facts of a story as reported don't add up or make sense, Q will use a math equation to suggest that the facts must be carefully evaluated or interpreted logically.

41 — The 41st President of the United States; George H.W. Bush.

4-10-20 — Initials of Donald John Trump when the numbers are replaced with the corresponding letters of the alphabet.

4chan — An internet message board where users can post anonymously.

5:5 — "Five by five" is military jargon signifying loud and clear, or understood. Radio transmissions are rated for signal clarity and strength on a scale from 1-5 with 1 being the lowest and 5 being the highest. 5:5 indicates the signal is loud and clear.

5 Eyes or **Five Eyes** or **FVEY**   A multilateral intelligence-sharing alliance that includes Australia, Canada, New Zealand, the United Kingdom and the United States.

7 Dwarves — According to the Michael Kilian article Spy vs. Spy published in 2000 by *The Chicago Tribune*, the CIA has seven supercomputers named after the seven dwarves; Doc, Dopey, Bashful, Grumpy, Sneezy, Sleepy and Happy.

7th Floor — There are two possible decodes. According to an October 17th, 2016 article published by *The New York Post*, "The 7th Floor" was a group of U.S. State Department officials who met regularly on the 7th floor of the Harry S. Truman Building in Washington, D.C. The group's activities came to light in the fall of

2016 and appeared to have formed in support of Hillary Clinton during her email investigation. The FBI referred to them as the "shadow government" inside the State Department, which briefly attracted the attention of mainstream media. Most, if not all, members were terminated by Rex Tillerson in February of 2017. Depending on context, "7th Floor" can represent the upper echelon of the FBI.

8chan — An internet message board where users can post anonymously.

8kun — An internet message board where users can post anonymously. Created in 2019 after 8chan was deplatformed.

11.3 — The date of November 3rd. There is a second decode. The initials "KC" when the numbers are replaced with the corresponding letters of the alphabet. KC represents Kevin Clinesmith, the former FBI attorney who was the first person to be indicted and plead guilty in John Durham's investigation of the FISA applications submitted to surveil Carter Page.

11.4 — The date of November 4th.

15-10-5 or **[5] [10] [15]** — Q and the President occasionally post with predetermined time intervals (deltas) between their posts. In this case, Q had posted within five minutes of the President, and anons caught it. Q was directing them to find two past posts where the President tweeted a message 10 and 15 minutes from the time of his post.

44 — Barack Obama, the 44th President of the United States.

187 — California penal code for murder. Often found in criminal gang tattoos.

302 — An FD-302 form is used by FBI agents to summarize the interviews they conduct. A 302 contains information from the notes taken during the interview by the non-interviewing agent (there are supposed to be at least two agents present, one to interview and one to take notes).

470 Investigators — Department of Justice Inspector General Michael Horowitz is reported to have a staff of 470 investigators, attorneys and other personnel. Horowitz is coordinating with U.S. Attorney John Huber, giving Huber access to a staff considerably larger than that of a Special Counsel.

Glossary

702 — Section 702 of the Foreign Intelligence Surveillance Act. "This authority allows only the targeting, for foreign intelligence purposes, of communications of foreign persons who are located abroad."

2020_P election +1 — Q's way of indicating the day after the 2020 Presidential election or November 4th, 2020.

A321 — The Airbus A321 is a member of the Airbus A320 family of short-to medium-range, narrow-body, commercial passenger twin-engine jet airliners manufactured by Airbus.

A or A's — Agency, agencies, intelligence agencies.

ABC — May refer to the American Broadcasting Company but is also used as a generic reference to three letter agencies such as the FBI, DOJ, CIA, etc.

Adam Schiff — Democrat representative from California, and Chair of the House Select Committee on Intelligence.

Adm R — Admiral Michael Rogers, Director of the National Security Agency from 2014 to 2018. Rogers is a former U. S. Navy Admiral who served as the second commander of the U.S. Cyber Command.

ADV — Advantage

AF1 — Air Force 1, the call sign designator for the airplane in which the President of the United States travels, regardless of which particular airplane it happens to be.

AG — U.S. Attorney General

Agnes Nixon — TV soap opera pioneer who created the shows *One Life to Live* and *All My Children*.

AJ — Alex Jones, founder of InfoWars, a conservative media outlet operated by Free Speech Systems LLC.

AL — Senator Al Franken, who formerly represented the state of Minnesota, but resigned in 2017 after being accused of sexual impropriety and unwanted advances.

Alan — Alan Dershowitz, a lawyer, author, and Harvard law professor. Although he is a registered Democrat, Dershowitz has supported President Trump against those who have criticized him.

Alice — Hillary Clinton, as she was referred to in emails from Marty Torrey (published by *WikiLeaks*), who went by the moniker "Hatter."

Alice and Wonderland — A signature phrase that Q helped anons decode. Alice is Hillary Clinton. Wonderland is Saudi Arabia. Q says Saudi Arabia has been the source of funding for many U.S. politicians.

Alphabet — The parent company of Google, YouTube, and others subsidiaries.

AL-Q — Al-Qaeda, a militant Sunni Islamist organization founded in 1988 by Osama bin Laden.

AM — Andrew McCabe, Deputy Director of the FBI from February 2016 to January 2018. Later, McCabe became Acting Director of the FBI briefly—May 9th to August 2nd, 2017—after Director James Comey was fired, but McCabe then returned to his Deputy Director position until he was fired by Jeff Sessions in March of 2018.

Amanda Renteria — A political aide who has worked for U.S. Senators Dianne Feinstein and Debbie Stabenow. In 2018, she announced her candidacy for Governor of California but lost in the primary to Gavin Newsom.

Amb — Ambassador

AMB Matlock — Ambassador Jack F. Matlock Jr. was appointed by President Reagan to be the U.S. ambassador to USSR. Matlock has defended the Trump's transition team's contacts with Russian officials as normal diplomatic relations.

anarchy 99 — A reference to the fictional anarchist group and main antagonist of the 2002 film xXx.

Anderson Cooper — CNN News Anchor who previously served as chief international correspondent for Channel One News, where he reported and produced his own stories. Cooper graduated from Yale University in 1989 with a BA in political science. During college, he spent two summers as an intern at the Central Intelligence Agency.

Angela Dorothea Kasner — Angela Dorothea Merkel neé Kasner, Chancellor of the country of Germany.

Anne Wojcicki — The co-founder and CEO of 23andMe, a genetic testing company. She is married to Sergey Brin, the co-founder of Google. Her sister is Susan Wojcicki, the CEO of YouTube.

Anon or **Autist** — Anonymous people who monitor and post messages on 4chan, 8chan, or 8kun. Many are researchers. The autist label refers to the fact that "autists" can become hyper-focused on their research.

Antifa — An American militant movement that embraces a far-left political ideology. Members employ a variety of tactics, including online activism, damaging personal property, inflicting physical violence, and harassing those they deem to be fascists, racists, or politically far-right.

APACHE — A term that has multiple meanings. It may refer to the internet domain that hosts SecureDrop, a platform that journalists use to communicate anonymously with their sources. It could also refer to the open source software used on computer servers. Or it may refer to Apache Co. (NYSE:APA), an oil and exploration company. The Rothschild's Family Trust divested 30 percent of their interest in the company in late January of 2018.

ARM or **ARM/MSM** — The context of its use would seem to indicate ARM is a group connected to the mainstream media, who oppose the agenda of President Trump. (Q has not confirmed an exact decode.)

Article — Typically refers to the articles of impeachment brought against President Trump by members of Congress in January of 2020.

As the World Turns — A television soap opera that aired on CBS for 54 years. When President John F. Kennedy was assassinated in 1963, the news story about the assassination interrupted the show's broadcast.

AS — There are three possible decodes. It has been confirmed as the initials of Antonin Scalia, the Supreme Court Justice, who died mysteriously in 2016.

Alternately, it may refer to Adam Schiff, the Democrat representative from California. In November of 2018, Abigail Spanberger was elected as the representative of Virginia's 7th congressional district. Spanberger is a former CIA agent. Context determines the best decode.

ASAP — As soon as possible.

ATL — Hartsfield-Jackson Atlanta International Airport

ATL -> IAD — Atlanta Airport to Dulles International Airport

AUS — The country of Australia.

Autist or **Anon** — Anonymous people who monitor and post messages on 4chan, 8chan, or 8kun. Many are researchers. The autist label refers to the fact that "autists" can become hyper-focused on their research.

AW — Anthony Weiner, disgraced ex-congressman from New York who served time in prison, and former husband of Huma Abedin.

Awan — Family name of the Pakistani brothers Imran, Abid and Jamal, who operated an IT company that was hired by more than 40 Democratic members of Congress. Imran Awan pled guilty to bank fraud charges but a Department of Justice case regarding him is currently open.

AZ — Arizona, a state in the U.S.

B2 or **B(2)** — The B-2 Spirit, also known as the Stealth Bomber. An American military bomber featuring radar-evading aircraft shapes and built with radar-resistant materials. Q has used the term to refer to someone who seems unthreatening but is working covertly.

Bad actor — A person who has engaged in criminal acts or corrupt behavior.

Bakers — Slang term for anons who assemble 4chan, 8chan, or 8kun posts (crumbs) into threads (breads) for discussion.

BB — U.S. Attorney General William (Bill) Barr.

Glossary

BC — Bill Clinton, 42nd President of the United States from 1993 to 2001.

BDT — Several possibilities: Blunt & Direct Time, Bangladeshi Taka (Bangladesh's currency). Bangladeshi Terrorist or a Bulk Data Transfer.

Betsy D or **Betsy DeVos** — Secretary of Education under President Trump, and sister of Erik Prince.

Biblefag — Slang term for a 4chan, 8chan, or 8kun user who posts scripture from the Bible.

Biden — Joe Biden, 2020 Democratic candidate for U.S. President.

BIDEN/CHINA — Robert Biden (son of former Vice President Joe Biden) partnered with John Kerry's stepson, Chris Heinz, to form Rosemont Seneca Partners, LLC. The firm signed a billion-dollar deal with the government-owned Bank of China following a diplomatic trip to that country by then-Vice President Joe Biden.

Bilderberg Group — Variously referred to as the Bilderberg Group, Bilderberg conference, Bilderberg meetings or Bilderberg Club, it is a group of 120 to 150 elite members of society including individuals from governments, business, media, and academia from Europe and the United States, which meets annually to promote the concept of "Atlanticism," which is an agenda that supports the mutual interests of Europe and the U.S.

Bill Priestap — Director of FBI Counterintelligence from 2015 to 2018.

Black ops — Black budget operations. Government operations (typically military or intelligence) that are not publicly acknowledged and not under congressional oversight. Some of these operations are funded through the official federal budget. Some are funded by siphoning money from approved programs, some by money made through illegal activities, and some are funded privately.

Blackwater — Blackwater USA is an American private military company founded in 1997 by former Navy SEAL officer Erik Prince. It was renamed as Xe Services in 2009 and is now known as Academi after the company was acquired by a group of private investors.

Blizzard — Activision Blizzard, Inc. is an American video game holding company based in Santa Monica, California.

BLM — Black Lives Matter. (Not to be confused with the Bureau of Land Management, a U.S. government agency)

Blockade — Q indicated that Robert Mueller's investigation into 2016 election interference was designed by the enemies of Donald Trump to serve as a blockade to his success.

BO — There are three confirmed decodes: Bruce Ohr (former U.S. Associate Deputy Attorney General), former President Barack Obama, or Board Owner.

BOB — Robert Mueller, former FBI Director who served as Special Counsel in the 2016 Trump-Russia investigation.

BOD — Board of Directors

B_Ohr — Bruce Ohr, the former Associate Deputy Attorney General who was demoted for his role in the surveillance of the 2016 Trump campaign.

Bolton — An American attorney, political commentator, and Republican consultant. Bolton was President Trump's National Security Advisor from March 2018 until September 2019. He also served as the U.S. Ambassador to the United Nations from August 2005 to December 2006.

BOOM — As in "Lower the Boom." Chastisement, punishment, or to deliver a knockout punch.

Boris — UK Prime Minister Boris Johnson.

Bots — Internet 'crawler' programs used to find and analyze data and run coded routines. May also be used as a derogatory term for people with a certain belief system, i.e., "Russian bots" or "Soros' bots."

Bottom to top — An order of operations that begins at the lowest level and proceeds toward the upper levels. These operations, because of their nature, take time to complete.

Glossary

BP — There are two decodes: Border Patrol, or Bill Priestap (FBI former Chief of Counterintelligence).

Bridge — A term found in Q's posts that indicates someone who acts as a go-between for others. It has also been used in at least one post that discusses a "central" social media algorithm that helps track users. The word has other uses that are still not confirmed by Q.

Bring the thunder — Artillery/aircraft controller term for final authorization of a fire/bombing mission.

Bruce Ohr — Former U.S. Associate Deputy Attorney General, who was demoted for his role in the surveillance of President Trump. Husband of Nellie Ohr, an employee of Fusion GPS.

Bump — A comment that forces a conversation thread to rise to the top of a particular board.

Burner phone — A cheap, disposable phone used by those who do not wish to be tracked by intelligence agencies.

BUZZF — Buzzfeed, an American internet media company.

C19 — COVID-19.

C_A — Central Intelligence Agency, A civilian foreign intelligence service of the U.S. federal government.

CA — In most cases, it refers to California, but when used in a stringer with Uranium One (U1), it refers to Canada.

Call the ball — A phrase derived from U.S. Navy terminology for a naval aviator confirming he has the optical landing aids in sight prior to landing on an aircraft carrier. In Q's vernacular, it signifies committing to a course of action.

Carter Page — Briefly served as a staffer on candidate Donald Trump's 2016 Presidential campaign. Page became the target of an FBI investigation as a possible foreign agent, and then became the center of a controversy surrounding the surveillance of Trump's campaign.

Castle — Secret Service code name for the Executive Mansion or White House.

CBTS — Calm before the storm.

CC — Chelsea Clinton, daughter of Bill and Hillary Clinton.

CCP — Usually stands for Chinese Communist Party, but has also been used as an acronym for Control and Command Positions.

CD — Camp David; a 125-acre country retreat for the President of the United States.

CDC — U.S. Centers for Disease Control

CF — The William Jefferson Clinton Foundation

CF-i — The Department of Justice's investigation of the Clinton Foundation.

CFR — Council on Foreign Relations, a United States non-profit think tank specializing in U.S. foreign policy and international affairs.

CHAI — Clinton Health Access Initiative. In 2010, the Clinton Foundation's HIV/AIDS Initiative became a separate non-profit organization called the Clinton Health Access Initiative (CHAI).

Chair — Likely a reference to what the Catholic Church considers to be the throne of St. Peter on which the current Pope sits.

Chatter — Conversations between politicians, media and intelligence operatives that are detected by agencies like the NSA.

CIA — Central Intelligence Agency, a civilian foreign intelligence service of the U.S. federal government.

C-Info — Confidential or Classified Information.

Civ — Two possibilities: civilian, or civil.

Glossary

Clapper — James Clapper, former Director of National Intelligence under Barack Obama.

CLAS or [CLAS 1-99] — Q has access to both classified and non-classified information. These terms refer to the names of people, agencies, and organizations that are currently classified.

Clock — Some believe the word clock is a reference to a clock diagram—the "Q clock" that is said to pinpoint and predict events in Q's mission. This clock diagram was created by an anon and has been posted on Q's board many times. Anons have asked for confirmation, but Q has not yet confirmed the clock diagram.

Note: My theory about references to a "clock" takes into consideration that Q and the President post close to each other in time—often less than ten minutes apart. A clock is necessary to track the time intervals (deltas), showing the relationships between their posts. Graphics can then be made showing the time intervals.

Clowns — The U.S. Central Intelligence Agency.

CLOWN DIR — Former CIA Director John Brennan

CM — CodeMonkey, the administrator who provided technical support for Q's board on 8chan, and the current administrator of 8kun.

Coats — Dan Coats, former Director of National Intelligence under President Donald Trump.

CoC — Two confirmed decodes: Chain of Command, and Chain of Custody.

Cohen — Michael Cohen, former personal attorney for Donald Trump.

Cohn — Gary Cohn, President Trump's former Chief Economic Advisor.

Color Revolution — A technique of overthrowing governments by the use of insurgency tactics—generally both violent and non-violent.

COMM or COMMS — Different possibilities depending on context. An abbreviation for communications, committee, or community.

comp-to-comp — Computer-to-computer.

Con — Confidence game: a swindle in which the mark, or victim, is defrauded after his or her trust (confidence) has been won.

Conf —Abbreviation for confirm, confirmation, configuration.

Corsi — Jerome Corsi is an author and political commentator. He was an avid Q supporter early in the mission but became the center of a controversy in the spring of 2018 when he claimed that Q had been compromised, and Q's posts could no longer be trusted.

CoS — Chief of Staff.

Co's —An abbreviation for companies.

Crop or **[crop]** — A euphemism used by Q to taunt former FBI Director James Comey about his pending prosecution. (Comey has often posted photos of himself standing in a cornfield.)

Crossfire Hurricane — The codename for the FBI's counterintelligence investigation of Donald Trump's campaign prior to the appointment of Special Counsel Robert Mueller.

CrowdStrike — A tech company contracted by the Democratic National Committee to investigate their computer system for alleged hacking during the 2016 Presidential election.

Crumb — Slang term for a single post on 4chan, 8chan, or 8kun. Crumbs, when brought together, make a bread (thread).

Cruz or **[-Cruz]** — U.S. Senator Ted Cruz

CS — Several confirmed decodes: Senator Charles Schumer, former British spy Christopher Steele, or the tech firm CrowdStrike that was used by the Democratic National Committee. Context determines the best decode.

CV — COVID-19

Glossary

C wave2 — A predicted second wave of the COVID virus.

C Wray — Christopher Wray, Director of the FBI who began serving in that capacity in 2017. From 2003 to 2005, he was the Assistant Attorney General in charge of the Criminal Division in the George W. Bush administration.

cycling 5s — Cycling every 5 seconds. Used in reference to Twitter and Facebook algorithms.

D5 — The metric used to rate the potential danger an avalanche poses on a scale from D1-D5, with D5 being most severe. Q uses it as a metaphor to convey the idea that a coming avalanche of justice will devastate corrupt people.

D or D's — Democrats

DA — District Attorney

Dafna Linzer — Since October of 2016, she has been the managing editor of NBC/MSNBC politics.

DAG — U.S. Deputy Attorney General

Dan — Usually a reference to Dan Scavino, the White House Deputy Chief of Staff for Communications and Director of Social Media.

DARPA — The U.S. Defense Department's Advanced Research Projects Agency. Q has suggested that DARPA developed much of the technology used by major social media platforms.

David Laufman — Former Chief of the U.S. Justice Department's Counterintelligence and Export Control Section.

DC — Washington, District of Columbia.

DC-CAP — Washington D.C., Capitol of the United States.

DDoS or **DDOS** — Distributed Denial of Service, a malicious attack used to take down a website or network by causing server overload. "Distributed" means the attack comes from multiple users and machines that overtax a site's resources.

Dead Cat Bounce — An investing term for a temporary recovery in a prolonged decline or bear market that is followed by the continuation of the downtrend. The name "dead cat bounce" illustrates the idea that even a dead cat will bounce if it falls far enough and fast enough.

Declas or **DECLASS** — The declassification of documents that may shed light on corruption when revealed.

Deep Dream — A reference to a Jason Bourne film in which a social media company named Deep Dream gathered personal information from subscribers and secretly funneled it to the Central Intelligence Agency.

Deep State — A term used for entrenched politicians, bureaucrats, and others who have their own policy agendas in government, and work to guard and maintain their positions of power and control. Therefore the status quo never seems to change no matter who is elected by the people.

DefCon — Defense Condition which is indicated by a number 1 through 5. DefCon 5 is a state of low alert. DefCon1 is a state of high alert. Q has used the term in some unorthodox ways. Look for context to determine the correct application.

Delta — Several possible uses: The U.S. Defense Department uses four conditions to indicate the relative level of a terrorist threat (Threatcon). Alpha is the lowest Threatcon level, bravo is higher and delta is the highest. In chemistry, delta (Δ) is used to indicate the change in a system during a reaction. For fighter pilots, it indicates a change to a later time, either minutes or hours depending on the context. ("Delta 10 on your recovery time" means the jet is now scheduled to land 10 minutes later.) In most of Q's posts, the term "delta" indicates the time interval between one of Q's posts and a tweet by the President.

DE_POTUS — Democratically elected President of the United States.

D/ F — Domestic and Foreign.

DF — Dianne Feinstein, a Democrat U.S. Senator from California.

DHS — U.S. Department of Homeland Security, which is a cabinet department of the U.S. federal government with responsibilities in public security.

Glossary

Digital Battleground — Q's term that describes a war of information being waged on the internet, and specifically—on social media.

DJT — Donald John Trump, the 45th President of the United States. Before entering politics, he was a businessman and television personality.

DL — Download

Dla Piper — The law firm that happened to employ Peter Comey, the brother of disgraced former FBI Director James Comey.

DNC — Democratic National Committee, the governing body for the United States Democratic Party.

DNC BREACH — In 2016, files from the Democratic National Committee were made public. The incident was widely attributed to a Russian hacking operation, but Q has suggested the information was obtained by a DNC staffer.

DNI — U.S. Director of National Intelligence.

DOD — U.S. Department of Defense, which is part of the Executive Branch of the federal government that handles functions of national security.

DOE — U.S. Department of Energy, a cabinet-level department of the federal government, concerned with energy and safe handling of nuclear material.

DOJ — U.S. Department of Justice (also known as the Justice Department), which is a federal executive department of the U.S. government responsible for the enforcement of the law and administration of justice in the U.S.

Donna — Donna Brazile, who served as the interim Chair of the Democratic National Committee in 2016 after the resignation of Debbie Wasserman Schultz.

Dopey — In a tweet, Donald Trump referred to Saudi Prince Alwaleed bin Talal as "Dopey Prince Alwaleed." Q has also referred to Alwaleed as Dopey.

DOSSIER — A collection of documents assembled by former British spy Christopher Steele, used to obtain a warrant to surveil Carter Page and the Trump campaign.

DrudgeR — The Drudge Report, a news aggregation service.

DT — Donald Trump

Durham — John Durham, U.S. Attorney from Connecticut. Tasked by former Attorney General Jeff Sessions to investigate government corruption.

DWS — Debbie Wasserman Schultz, a Representative from Florida who resigned as chair of the DNC after emails were published by that revealed DNC staff favoring Clinton over Sanders.

E — Two confirmed decodes: The rapper known as Eminem, or emergency.

Eagle — Secret Service code name for President Bill Clinton.

EAM LOYALISTS — In the U.S. military's strategic nuclear weapon command and control system, an Emergency Action Message (EAM) is a preformatted message directing nuclear-capable forces to execute specific Major Attack Options (MAOs) or Limited Attack Options (LAOs) in a nuclear war. "EAM Loyalsts" would be members of the military who would receive such a message and intend to keep their oath and serve their country faithfully.

EBS — Emergency Broadcast System

EC — This usually signifies Electronic Communication, as in email, instant messaging, or other communications. In more recent posts, it refers to Eric Ciaramella, a CIA analyst and former National Security Council staffer. Ciaramella is believed to have filed the whistleblower complaint used to impeach Donald Trump.

Ed O'Callaghan — The former Principal Associate Deputy Attorney General for Rod Rosenstein.

EG — Abbreviation for Evergreen, Hillary Clinton's Secret Service code name.

EH — Eric Holder, former U.S. Attorney General under Barrack Obama.

EM — Elon Musk, CEO of Tesla and SpaceX.

Glossary

EMP — Electromagnetic Pulse

EMS — Emergency Messaging System

EO — Presidential Executive Order

Epstein — Jeffrey Epstein, an American financier and convicted child sex offender who died in his jail cell in 2019 while awaiting trial.

Epstein Island — Little Saint James Island, an approximately 75-acre island in the U.S. Virgin Islands, owned by American financier and convicted child sex offender Jeffrey Epstein from 1998 until his death in 2019.

Erik Prince — Former U.S. Navy SEAL officer best known for founding the government services and security company, Blackwater USA. He served as its CEO until 2009. Prince supported Donald Trump in his bid for President.

ES — Two confirmed decodes: Eric Schmidt (ex-CEO of Alphabet/Google) or Edward Snowden, a former CIA employee and NSA contractor. Snowden is usually indicated by @snowden but on rare occasions by ES. Context determines which is correct.

ETA — Estimated time of arrival.

EU — European Union

Evergreen — Hillary Clinton's Secret Service code name.

Exec — An abbreviation for executive or execute.

Eyes in the SKY — Drone or satellite surveillance.

Eyes On — To watch or observe.

Ezra Cohen-Watnick — National security advisor to the U.S. Attorney General, and a former Senior Director for Intelligence Programs for the United States National Security Council (NSC).

F2F — Face-to-face meeting.

F9 — Two uses: SpaceX Falcon 9 is a two-stage medium-lift space launch vehicle. F9 is also a Facebook surveillance algorithm.

Facebook — A popular social network founded on February 4th, 2004—the same day the Pentagon's DARPA Lifelog Project was shut down. Lifelog was designed to track the same life events as Facebook.

Fag — Slang term for an anon. It is sometimes combined with areas of interest, i.e. biblefag, planefag, lawfag, etc.

Fakewood — Hollywood

Fantasy Land — A Q signature indicating a truth that is too wild for the average person to believe. Cognitive dissonance is caused by information that challenges a programmed way of thinking.

FAQ — Frequently asked question.

Farm — A nickname for the CIA's training facility, Camp Peary, near Williamsburg, Virginia.

FB — Facebook

F + D — Foreign and Domestic

FED — Federal Reserve System, a private banking corporation that controls the U.S. money supply.

FED G — Federal Government

FEMA — U.S. Federal Emergency Management Agency

FF — False Flag. A secret operation that is intended to deceive. The deception creates the appearance that a particular party, group, or nation is responsible for some type of activity, while the actual source of the activity is concealed. The term originally referred to pirate ships that flew flags of countries as a disguise to prevent their victims from fleeing or preparing for battle. Sometimes the flag would remain, and the blame for the attack would be laid incorrectly on another country.

Glossary

FIFTH COLUMN — A group within a country that are secretly sympathetic to or are working with its enemies.

FISA — The Foreign Intelligence Surveillance Act, which permits the surveillance of foreign citizens or U.S. citizens suspected of being foreign agents.

Five Eyes — Often abbreviated FVEY, it is an intelligence-sharing alliance that includes Australia, Canada, New Zealand, the United Kingdom, and the United States.

FLOTUS — an abbreviation for First Lady of the United States; usually refers to Melania Trump.

Flynn — Retired Lieutenant General Michael Flynn, who served as the Director of U.S. Defense Intelligence Agency.

FOIA — The Freedom of Information Act. It allows individuals to request government documents on particular subjects and requires compliance within certain guidelines.

Follow the Pen — A pen photograph has appeared in a number of Q's posts. Sometimes the images precede a Presidential Executive Order or declassification of documents.

Fox & Friends — A weekday morning news show on *Fox News* television channel.

Fox Three — Military aviator jargon for firing an active radar-guided air-to-air missile.

Future Marker — A reference in a post by Q intended to mark a topic that will be discussed in greater detail at a future time.

Future proves past — A phrase suggesting that information contained in a current post will be proven true at a future time.

FVEY — See Five Eyes.

G — Google

Game Theory — The study of conflict and cooperation by opponents within a competitive game environment.

Gang of 8 — A term used to describe the eight leaders in the United States Congress who are briefed on classified intelligence matters. It includes the leaders of both parties from the Senate and House of Representatives, and the chairs and ranking minority members of both the Senate and House Intelligence Committees.

Gardens by the Bay — A nature park in central Singapore, adjacent to the Marina Reservoir. Kim Jong-un explored the park on his first night in Singapore preceding the Summit meeting with President Trump on June 11th, 2018.

GCHQ — An acronym for the Government Communications Headquarters, an intelligence and security organization responsible for providing signals intelligence (SIGINT) and information to the UK government and armed forces.

General K — President Trump's former Chief of Staff General John F. Kelly.

GEO or **geo-location** — A reference to geographic location.

GEO-T or **GEO-T/L** — Geological tracking, and location. Tracking a person's location by using global positioning satellites.

GEOTUS — Acronym for God-Emperor of the United States. A meme used to aggravate those who despise Donald Trump.

GHWB — George Herbert Walker Bush, the 41st President of the United States.

Gina Haspel — Director of the CIA under President Trump.

GITMO — Guantanamo Bay Naval Base, a military prison and detention camp.

Giuliani — Former New York City Mayor Rudy Giuliani.

GJ — Grand Jury.

Gloria V — Gloria Vanderbilt, an American artist, author, actress, fashion designer, heiress, and socialite.

Glossary

GNP — Gross National Product.

Godfather III — A Q signature that connects posts containing this phrase to a film from 1990 about the Corleone crime family's involvement with the Vatican.

GOOG — Google

Great Awakening — A future event where society at large becomes aware of the reality of institutional corruption.

GREEN_CASTLE — Q confirmed this was a reference to the U.S. Army Corps of Engineers who have an office in Green Castle, Indiana.

GS — George Soros, a hedge fund billionaire who is known for using his wealth to fund his own brand of political activism. Recipients of his philanthropy appreciate his money, but those who oppose his political views see him as a creator of chaos around the world—a destabilizing force on economies and societies. Some countries have either banned Soros or restricted his organizations. These countries include Pakistan, Poland, Turkey, Russia, Soros' home country of Hungary, and the Philippines. The Israeli government has said Soros is not welcome there.

GSA — General Services Administration. An independent agency of the U.S. government that helps manage and support federal agencies.

Guccifer 2.0 — An internet persona who claimed to be the hacker(s) who gained unauthorized access to the Democratic National Committee (DNC) computer network and then leaked its documents to *WikiLeaks*.

G v E/R v W — Good versus evil. Right versus wrong.

GWB — Former U.S. President George W. Bush.

GZ — Ground Zero

H — Multiple possibilities. Depending on the context, H could mean either Haiti, U.S. House of Representatives, or in rare cases, Hillary Clinton, who is known to sign letters and emails with the letter H.

Hannity intruder — Sean Hannity's wife found a man trespassing in their home on Long Island. The intruder claimed to be writing a book about the *Fox News* host and was arrested.

Hatter — Marty Torrey, as he was referred to in emails from Hillary Clinton (published by *WikiLeaks*), who went by the nickname "Alice."

H-BIDEN — Hunter Biden, the son of 2020 Presidential candidate Joe Biden.

Hillary Clinton — Former Secretary of State under Barack Obama. Democratic Presidential candidate in 2016. Wife of President William Jefferson Clinton.

Hive-Mind — The ability of anons and researchers to coordinate their work, similar to how a bee hive operates.

HK — Hong Kong

Holder — Eric Holder, former U.S. Attorney General under Barrack Obama.

Honeypot — A scheme used to lure people into behaviors that are unethical, immoral, or illegal. Their participation can be recorded and used as leverage to control them.

Hops — FISA surveillance allows the collection of information on individuals in the targeted person's *immediate* circle of contacts. It also allows surveillance of other people who are *in communication with* the immediate circle of contacts. In this way, surveillance "hops" or acts as a "leapfrog" from a small circle of contacts to larger ones, extending a broader surveillance net.

HRC — Hillary Clinton, former Secretary of State under Barack Obama. Democratic Presidential candidate in 2016. Wife of former President William Jefferson Clinton.

H-relief — Haiti earthquake relief.

H Report — One of several reports released by the U.S. Department of Justice Inspector General Michael Horowitz.

HS — U.S. Department of Homeland Security

Glossary

Huma — Huma Abedin, Hillary Clinton's Chief of Staff, and ex-wife of Anthony Weiner.

HUMA — Harvard University Muslim Alumni

Hunter — Q often uses this as a euphemism for those who are hunting criminals and bringing them to justice. It can also refer to Hunter Biden, the trouble-prone son of former U.S. Vice President Joe Biden.

Hunt for Red October — Multiple meanings including, but not limited to, the film by that title and a steel plant in Stalingrad, Russia, which appears on a CIA document, for which Q provided a link. Note: Q removed "the Hunt for," and in October of 2018, a new theme "Red October" appeared.

Hussein — Barack Hussein Obama, the 44th President of the United States.

Hussein's PL — Barack Obama's Presidential Library

HW — Hollywood

H-wood — Hollywood

I — The letter I has been used at least once to refer to criminal indictments.

IBOR — Internet Bill of Rights, a set of ideas proposed by California Representative Ro Khanna that would guarantee the rights of internet users.

IC — Intelligence Community

ICBM — Intercontinental Ballistic Missile

ICE — U.S. Immigration and Customs Enforcement.

ID/IDEN — Identification, or to identify an individual.

IG — Inspector General. Every U.S. government agency has an Inspector General. In most cases, the reference is to the Department of Justice Inspector General Michael Horowitz.

ILS — Instrument Landing System. Radio signals are transmitted from a runway and are intercepted by aircraft that use them as a guide for landing. Used by Q in discussions with anons to help build camaraderie.

In-Q-Tel — A venture capital firm that invests in tech companies for the sole purpose of keeping the CIA and other intelligence agencies equipped with the latest in information technology. To those acquainted with the industry, the name "In-Q-Tel" is a reference to Q, the fictional inventor who supplied technology to James Bond.

Insurance Policy — According to publicly released text messages between FBI agent Peter Strzok and FBI attorney Lisa Page in 2016, a plan was developed to prevent Donald Trump from being elected. A backup plan (an insurance policy) was put in place to remove him from office if he were to be elected.

Intel Ops —Intelligence operations.

Intelligence A — Intelligence Agency

IP —Internet protocol address.

IP-Ghost — Using a device or software to conceal your IP address.

IRL — In real life, as opposed to online.

IRON EAGLE — A 1986 movie starring Lou Gossett Jr. about a retired Air Force Colonel and an 18-year-old whose father had been shot down in the Middle East and was sentenced to death. The two men obtained a pair of F-16 fighter jets and managed to fly to the Middle East for a rescue mission for the young man's father. Iron Eagle is a Q signature.

IRS — U.S. Internal Revenue Service, a government agency that is a bureau of the Department of the Treasury.

ISIS — Islamic State in Iraq and Syria. Listed as a terrorist group by the U.S.

Ism — A term Q uses to describe in generic terms, ideas such as racism, fascism, totalitarianism, etc.

Glossary

JA — Julian Assange, founder of *WikiLeaks,* a watchdog organization that publishes leaked documents.

Jack — Jack Dorsey, CEO of the social media platform, Twitter. He is also the CEO of the mobile payment processing company Square.

James Alefantis — Named in GQ magazine as one of Washington D.C.'s 50 most influential people. He is an American chef and restaurateur.

James Baker — Former FBI Chief Counsel.

James Comey — Former Director of the Federal Bureau of Investigation (FBI) who was fired by President Trump in 2017.

James Dolan — From 1999 to 2006, Dolan served with the U.S. Marines in the Iraq war. He helped develop SecureDrop, an open source whistleblower submission system that eventually came under the control of the Freedom of the Press Foundation. Dolan's death at the age of 36 on December 27th, 2017, was thought to be a suicide and was followed by the death of John Perry Barlow in February of 2018.

Jared Cohen — A businessman who serves as the CEO of Jigsaw (previously Google Ideas) and an Adjunct Senior Fellow at the Council on Foreign Relations (CFR). Previously, he served as a member of the Secretary of State's Policy Planning Staff and as an advisor to Condoleezza Rice and later, Hillary Clinton.

Jason Bourne — A fictional agent and hero in a series of books and films. Bourne was the subject of a CIA mind-control experiment that made him into the perfect asset for the Agency. Used by Q with the term Deep Dream to indicate how social media is used by the CIA to control the masses.

JB — At least two confirmed decodes: former FBI Chief Counsel James Baker, or former CIA Director John Brennan. Context determines the correct one.

JC — At least two confirmed decodes: former FBI Director James Comey, or former Director of National Intelligence James Clapper. Context determines the correct one.

J C or **J_C** — John P. Carlin, former Director of the National Security Division of the U.S. Department of Justice.

JCS — The U.S. Military's Joint Chiefs of Staff.

JD — Jack Dorsey, the CEO of Twitter, a social media platform, and the CEO of Square, a mobile payment processing company.

JFK — Two confirmed decodes: John Fitzgerald Kennedy, 35th President of the United States, or President Trump's former Chief of Staff General John F. Kelly.

JFK JR — John Fitzgerald Kennedy, Jr. was the son of the 35th President John F. Kennedy Sr. He was a lawyer, journalist, magazine publisher, and actor. Kennedy died on July 16th, 1999 (along with his wife, Carolyn, and sister-in-law Lauren Bessette) when his small plane crashed into the Atlantic Ocean near Martha's Vineyard.

Jim Jordan — Representative from Ohio's 4th congressional district and member of the House Freedom Caucus. He has been the ranking member of the House Oversight Committee since 2019.

Jim Rybicki — Former FBI Chief of Staff.

JK — Two confirmed decodes: In Q's earlier posts, JK refers to Jared Kushner, senior advisor to his father-in-law, President Donald Trump. In later Q posts, JK refers to John Kerry, Secretary of State under Barack Obama.

JL — John Legend, singer, songwriter, musician, actor, and philanthropist. Legend participated in a telethon to benefit Haiti victims.

John Durham — U.S. Attorney from Connecticut. Tasked by former Attorney General Jeff Sessions to investigate government corruption.

John M — John McCain, U.S. Senator from Arizona. He served as a senator from January 1987 until his death in 2018.

John McCain — U.S. Senator from Arizona who served from January 1987 until his death in 2018.

Glossary

Johnny — John Conyers, U.S. Representative from Michigan who resigned from Congress in 2017 after multiple allegations of sexual harassment. Now deceased, he was the longest-serving black member of Congress in history.

John P. Carlin — Former Director of the National Security Division of the U.S. Department of Justice.

John Perry Barlow — Poet and essayist, cattle rancher, and a cyber-libertarian, political activist, and lyricist for the Grateful Dead. Founding member of the Electronic Frontier Foundation and the Freedom of the Press Foundation. Barlow died in February, 2018.

Josh Campbell — Former FBI agent, appointed Special Assistant to former FBI Director James Comey. Contributor for CNN.

JP — John Podesta, White House Chief of Staff under President Bill Clinton, and Counselor to President Barack Obama. Chairman of Hillary Clinton's 2016 Presidential campaign. Currently serves as Chair of the Center for American Progress, a think tank based in Washington, D.C.

JPC — John P. Carlin, former Director of the National Security Division of the U.S. Department of Justice.

JS — John Solomon, investigative journalist, reporter, and Editor in Chief of *Just the News*.

K — Supreme Court Justice Brett Kavanaugh.

KANSAS — Mike Pompeo, former CIA director and current Secretary of State. Pompeo also served as a U.S. Congressman from Kansas.

Kashyap Patel — Indian American lawyer Kashyap "Kash" Patel, who was the primary author of the House Intelligence Committee memo that was critical of the FBI and Justice Department handling of the investigation into alleged collusion between Donald Trump and Russia.

KC — Kevin Clinesmith, a former FBI attorney who was the first person to be indicted and plead guilty in John Durham's investigation related to "Crossfire

Hurricane." Clinesmith admitted to altering an email used to obtain a warrant for broad surveillance of Carter Page, a U.S. citizen and member of the Trump campaign.

Kek — Laughter or amusement. Synonymous with "lol" (laughing out loud). Kek had its origins in World of Warcraft, where one faction's "lol" was translated as "kek" by the other.

Keith Raniere — Co-founder of NXIVM, a multi-level marketing company based near Albany, New York, that offered personal and professional development seminars through its "Executive Success Programs." NXIVM leaders were prosecuted for sexual abuse and sex trafficking of members.

Kerry — John Kerry, a former U.S. Senator and Secretary of State under President Barack Obama.

Kevin Clinesmith — Former FBI attorney who was the first person to be indicted and plead guilty in John Durham's investigation related to "Crossfire Hurricane." Clinesmith admitted to altering an email used to obtain a warrant for broad surveillance of Carter Page, a U.S. citizen and member of the Trump campaign.

Keystone — Several uses: decoded by Q to indicate the power given to average citizens when they're assisted by the President, the military, and its intelligence apparatus. Information is the *key*. The executive branch and military are the *stone*. Together, they form the *keystone*. Also refers to a trapezoidal-shaped building stone found at the apex of some arches and doorways.

Kill Chain — A military term that describes the structure of an attack. It consists of identifying a target, dispatching forces to the target, initiating an attack, and destruction of the target.

Kim — Kim Jong-un is a North Korean politician who has been the Supreme Leader of North Korea since 2011 and chairman of the Workers' Party of Korea since 2012.

KKK — Ku Klux Klan, a group that became a vehicle for southern post-Civil War resistance against freedmen and the Republican Party leaders who sought to

Glossary

establish equality for blacks. As a secret, masked vigilante group, the Klan aimed to restore white supremacy by using threats and violence, including murder.

Klaus Eberwein — A former Haitian government official who was found shot to death just before he was scheduled to expose Clinton Foundation fraud before an anti-corruption committee.

Knowingly — Used by Q as a reminder that many actions taken by corrupt people were not done negligently, but knowingly. Negligence is generally not prosecuted. Certain acts, when done knowingly, are.

LARP — Live Action Role Play. On 4chan, 8chan and 8kun, it refers to a phony.

Lawfag — A slang term for an anon who has a background in law.

LdR or LDR — Two possible decodes. Lord de Rothschild or Lynn de Rothschild (aka Lady de Rothschild)—both members of the Rothschild banking family.

Leapfrog — FISA surveillance allows the collection of information on individuals in the targeted person's *immediate* circle of contacts. It also allows surveillance of other people who are *in communication with* the immediate circle of contacts. In this way, surveillance "hops" or acts as a "leapfrog" from a small circle of contacts to larger ones, extending a broader surveillance net.

LifeLog Project — A project of DARPA, the Defense Department's research arm. The goal of the LifeLog Project was to get citizens to voluntarily provide their private information to a military database. The program ended on February 4th, 2004—the same day Facebook was launched.

Lisa Barsoomian — Former Assistant U.S. Attorney who once represented Bill Clinton. She is the wife of former Deputy Attorney General Rod Rosenstein.

Lisa Page — Former FBI attorney, and legal advisor to then-FBI Deputy Director Andrew McCabe. Page became the focus of media attention for her role in the surveillance of Donald Trump's 2016 Presidential campaign.

Little St. James Island — Little Saint James Island, an approximately 75-acre island in the U.S. Virgin Islands, owned by American financier and convicted child sex offender Jeffrey Epstein from 1998 until his death in 2019.

LL — Loretta Lynch, served as U.S. Attorney General under Barack Obama. Lynch came under scrutiny when she met secretly with former President Bill Clinton on a tarmac at an airport in Arizona during an active investigation of Hillary Clinton.

Locked on target — Military aircraft use radar to track or "lock" onto the position of other aircraft. As Q uses the term, it refers to corrupt people who are being tracked.

Login Devices — Various secure computers, tablets, or mobile phones that Q uses to connect to the internet to post messages.

LOOP — In most cases, a reference to Loop Capital Markets, a Chicago-based investment firm. There may be other uses.

Lord d R — Lord Jacob de Rothschild of the Rothschild banking family.

LOSBR — Line-of-sight beam riding. A technique of directing a missile to its target by aid of radar or a laser beam.

Lurk — To read a 4chan, 8chan, or 8kun board without posting a comment. Lurking is not only acceptable, but recommended. If you make a bad or unoriginal post, someone will likely ask you to "lurk more" (sometimes written "lurk moar") before posting again.

LV — Las Vegas, a city in Nevada.

LZ — Landing Zone. Q's references are typically to locations where a military aircraft land.

M — Used at least once to refer to Moloch, the biblical name of a Canaanite god associated with child sacrifice.

Mack — Allison Mack, a Hollywood actress who played the part of Chloe Sullivan in the TV show *Smallville*. Mack pleaded guilty to racketeering and conspiracy as a member of the NXIVM sex cult that was founded by Keith Raniere. As part of her guilty plea, Mack admitted to extortion and forced labor.

Glossary

Macron — Emmanuel Macron, elected President of France on May 7th, 2017.

MAGA — "Make America Great Again," Donald Trump's 2016 Presidential campaign slogan.

Maggie Haberman — White House correspondent for *The New York Times* and a former political analyst for CNN. Emails published by indicated that Haberman was particularly useful in releasing political talking points friendly to Hillary Clinton. She was also reported by to be one of many reporters who colluded with Hillary's campaign and the DNC during the 2016 election.

Maggie Nix — The daughter of Sarah Nixon and granddaughter of actress and TV soap opera writer and producer Agnes Nixon.

MagikBOT — A *Wikipedia* bot that makes automated or semi-automated edits to *Wikipedia* entries that would be difficult to do manually.

MAKE IT RAIN — Military jargon for the detonation of explosive ordnance (bomb), which sends a shower of debris on those who are nearby.

Manafort — Paul Manafort, a businessman, lobbyist, and member of Donald Trump's 2016 Presidential campaign. He was convicted of money laundering, tax evasion and failing to register as a foreign agent.

Mariah Sunshine Coogan — One of six people killed in a plane crash near Scottsdale, Arizona, on a flight to Las Vegas, Nevada, on April 9th, 2018.

Marina Abramovic — A Serbian performance artist mentioned in the John Podesta emails published by *WikiLeaks* drawing public attention to her "Spirit Cooking" art, as well as her relationships with political figures and celebrities.

Marine 1 — The President's helicopter operated by the U.S. Marines.

Marker — A reference in a post by Q intended to mark a topic that will be discussed in greater detail at a future time.

MAP — A graphic that displays Q's posts.

Master — The identity of the "Master" is uncertain. In a discussion about the Pope and the Rothschilds, Q wrote:

> The "Chair" serves the Master
> P = C.
> Who is the Master?

May — Theresa May, served as the Prime Minister of the United Kingdom and Leader of the Conservative Party from 2016 to 2019.

MB — Muslim Brotherhood, a political and military group based in Egypt. The government of Egypt banned the group and named it a terrorist organization.

MBS — Two decodes. Mohammad bin Salman, the Crown Prince of Saudi Arabia, Muslim reformer, and ally of Donald Trump. Depending on context, MBS can refer to Marina Bay Sands Hotel in Singapore.

McCabe — Andrew McCabe, Deputy Director of the FBI from February 2016 to January 2018. Later, McCabe became Acting Director of the FBI briefly—May 9th to August 2nd, 2017—after Director James Comey was fired, but McCabe then returned to his Deputy Director position until he was fired by Jeff Sessions in March of 2018.

Media Matters — Media Matters for America (MMfA) is a progressive tax-exempt, non-profit organization, with the stated mission of "comprehensively monitoring, analyzing, and correcting conservative misinformation in the U.S. media." MMfA was founded by political activist David Brock and is known for its aggressive criticism of conservative journalists and media outlets. Hillary Clinton and John Podesta were instrumental in helping form MMfA, which receives partial funding from George Soros.

Melissa Hodgman — Associate Director of Securities and Exchange Commission Enforcement Division. Wife of fired FBI Special Agent Peter Strzok.

MI — Military Intelligence

Memo — House Intelligence Committee 4-page memo on the FBI's FISA warrant against Trump campaign staffer Carter Page.

Glossary

Merkel — Angela Merkel, a politician who has served as the Chancellor of Germany since 2005.

MF — Retired Lieutenant General Michael Flynn, served as the National Security Advisor briefly under President Trump in 2017. Flynn became a target during the SpyGate scandal and entered a guilty plea under pressure from Special Counsel prosecutors. Previously, Flynn served as Director of the Defense Intelligence Agency for two years under the Obama administration and was forced out due to his criticism of Obama's policy on the Islamic State.

Michael Atkinson — Former Inspector General for the U.S. Intelligence Community. He was fired after his involvement was exposed in facilitating the whistleblower complaint that led to the House impeachment of President Trump.

Michael Avenatti — The attorney who represented Stormy Daniels in her lawsuit against President Trump. Q has not mentioned him by name but has posted links to his tweets and his website. Avenatti is currently facing charges in New York and California.

Michael Gaeta — The FBI's legal attaché in Rome, Italy.

Midnight Riders — A term Q adopted for anons in the summer of 2020, that symbolizes the patriotism of Paul Revere, who rode a horse at midnight to warn of the British plan to arrest Samuel Adams and John Hancock.

Midterm — A U.S. election held every fourth year when the office of the President is not on the ballot.

Midyear — Midyear Exam, the FBI's name for its investigation of Hillary Clinton's use of a private server in her home for email correspondence while she was Secretary of State.

Mika Brzezinski — MSNBC reporter and co-host of the weekday show *Morning Joe*, and daughter of Zbigniew Brzezinski (President Jimmy Carter's National Security Advisor.)

Mike Kortan — Former FBI Assistant Director for Public Affairs, an influential position that controlled media access. He also served under Robert Mueller in the 2016 Trump-Russia probe.

MIL brass — Military leaders

MIL-CIV Alliance — An informal alliance between members of the military and civilians in an effort to inform the public about the realities of corruption.

MIL SATs — Military Satellites

M-Institute — The McCain Institute for International Leadership, a Washington D.C. based think tank established in cooperation with Arizona State University.

Mitch McConnell — Mitch McConnell, U.S. Senator from Kentucky is also the Senate Majority Leader. Elected to that position unanimously by his Republican colleagues in 2014, 2016, and 2018, he is the longest-serving Senate Republican leader in the history of the United States.

MK_active — A suggestion from Q that the CIA's MK-Ultra mind control program is still active.

MKUltra — CIA mind-control project that involved the use of psychological experiments combined with the use of drugs.

ML — Marshal law, refers to a state where the military assumes control of civilian law enforcement duties.

MLK — The Reverend Martin Luther King, Jr. was the most influential black leader of the 1960s. He was a Baptist minister and an advocate of civil rights in America. He led the peaceful historical boycott of city buses in Montgomery, Alabama, in 1955. King was assassinated in 1968.

mm — Millions

MOAB — an acronym for Mother of All Bombs. The nickname for GBU-43/B Massive Ordnance Air Blast, which, weighing in at over 21,000 pounds, was the largest non-nuclear bomb ever used by the U.S. military. It was dropped on an ISIS-Khorasan camp in Afghanistan in April of 2017.

Moar — Slang term for "more" used on 4chan, 8chan, and 8kun.

Glossary

Mockingbird — Operation Mockingbird was a CIA operation where the agency recruited news reporters and their managers to disseminate propaganda for the purpose of controlling the masses.

mod — Sometimes refers to a moderator, but also the act of modifying.

Moloch — The biblical name of a Canaanite god associated with child sacrifice.

MOS — Mossad, an Israeli intelligence agency.

Mr. Contractor — Edward Snowden, a former CIA employee and NSA contractor who illegally leaked information about NSA surveillance programs to the press in 2013.

Mr. Ryan — Jack Ryan, a character from *The Hunt for Red October*.

MS-13 — Mara Salvatrucha, also known as MS-13, is a criminal gang that originated in Los Angeles, California, in the 1970s and 1980s. It was primarily comprised of and helped protect Salvadoran immigrants. The gang's influence has spread throughout the Western hemisphere and Europe. In 2012, the U.S. Department of the Treasury labeled the group a "transnational criminal organization," the first such designation for a U.S. street gang.

MSDNC — An acronym coined by conservative political pundits (also used by President Trump) to mock MSNBC's cable television channel. It comes from the idea that MSNBC is the propaganda arm or mouthpiece of the Democratic National Committee (DNC).

MSM — Mainstream Media

Mueller — Robert Mueller, former FBI Director and Special Counsel.

MW — Maxine Waters, a U.S. Representative from California who has served in Congress since 1991. A member of the Democrat Party, she chaired the Congressional Black Caucus from 1997 to 1999.

MX — The country of Mexico.

MYE — Midyear Exam, the FBI's name for its investigation of Hillary Clinton's use of a private server in her home for email correspondence while she was Secretary of State.

MZ — Mark Zuckerberg, founder, CEO, and controlling shareholder of the social media platform Facebook.

Nancy Pelosi — U.S. Representative from California and Speaker of the House of Representatives.

Nancy Salzman — President and co-founder of NXIVM, a multi-level marketing company based near Albany, New York, that offered personal and professional development seminars through its "Executive Success Programs." NXIVM leaders were prosecuted for sexual abuse and sex trafficking members.

NASA — U.S. National Aeronautics and Space Administration.

Natalia Veselnitskaya — A Russian attorney who gained notoriety for her meeting with Donald Trump Jr., Paul Manafort, and Jared Kushner prior to the 2016 Presidential election.

NATSEC or NAT SEC — National Security

N_C — National Security Council. Part of the Executive Office of the President of the United States. It is the principal forum used by the President for consideration of national security, military, and foreign policy matters with senior national security advisors and Cabinet officials.

NCSWIC — Two confirmed meanings; nothing can stop what is coming and National Council of Statewide Interoperability Coordinators.

NDA — Non-disclosure agreement. A commonly used legally-binding contract by which one or more parties agree not to disclose confidential information they have shared as a necessary part of doing business together.

Nellie Ohr — The wife of former Associate Deputy Attorney General Bruce Ohr. Both Ohrs have been implicated in the Obama administration's surveillance of the 2016 Trump Presidential campaign.

Glossary

Newfag — Slang term for new user on 4chan, 8chan, or 8kun.

NG — National Guard

NK — North Korea, also known as the Democratic People's Republic of Korea (DPRK).

NOFORN — Regarding the classification of information by the U.S. government, this designation (meaning "no foreign nationals") is applied to any information that may not be released to any non-U.S. citizen.

N_Ohr — Nellie Ohr, an employee of Fusion GPS, the firm that conducted research used in Christopher Steele's anti-Trump dossier. Wife of former Associate Deputy Attorney General Bruce Ohr. Steele's dossier was the source cited by the FBI in its FISA applications against Carter Page. The surveillance of Page allowed the Obama administration to spy on the 2016 Trump campaign.

No name — John McCain, U.S. Senator from Arizona. He served as a senator from January 1987 until his death in 2018.

Non_Civ — Two possibilities: non-civilian, or non-civil.

non Page — As it relates to FISA surveillance, Q hints these are FISA targeted individuals *other than* Carter Page.

Normalfag or **normie** — Slang term for normal members of society who don't share the same interests as those who commonly use 4chan, 8chan, or 8kun boards.

No Such Agency — National Security Agency (NSA) is a signals intelligence agency within the U.S. Department of Defense. It collects and analyzes electronic signals intelligence of interest to the security of the United States; protects all classified and sensitive information stored on government equipment; and contributes to the civilian use of cryptography and computer security measures.

NP — Usually refers to Nancy Pelosi, a U.S. Representative from California and Speaker of the House of Representatives. In a couple of cases (related to George Soros), it stands for nonprofit.

NPO — Non-Profit Organization

NR — Nuclear Reactor

NSA — National Security Agency is a signals intelligence agency within the U.S. Department of Defense. It collects and analyzes electronic signals intelligence of interest to the security of the U.S. and protects all classified and sensitive information stored on government information technology equipment. In addition, the NSA supports and contributes to the civilian use of cryptography and computer security measures.

NSC — National Security Council. Part of the Executive Office of the President of the United States. It is the principal forum used by the President for consideration of national security, military, and foreign policy matters with senior national security advisors and Cabinet officials.

Nunes — Devin Nunes, U.S. Representative from California and ranking member of the House Intelligence Committee.

NV — Natalia Veselnitskaya, a Russian attorney who gained notoriety for her meeting with Donald Trump Jr., Paul Manafort, and Jared Kushner prior to the 2016 Presidential election. Questions arose over how and why she was permitted entrance into the U.S. under President Obama's administration.

NWO — New World Order, sometimes referred to as a one-world government. A governmental concept where individual nations surrender their political sovereignty to the will of a centralized world governmental power.

NXIVM — A multi-level marketing company based near Albany, New York, that offered personal and professional development seminars through its "Executive Success Programs." NXIVM leaders were prosecuted for sexual abuse and sex trafficking of the group's members.

NYC — New York City

NYT — *The New York Times*, an American newspaper founded in 1851.

o7 — Used as an online salute. The letter o symbolizes a head. The number 7 is a hand in position to salute.

Glossary

OCONUS lures — Oconus = Outside Contiguous United States. Lures = spies. The term was found in text messages between FBI agent Peter Strzok and attorney Lisa Page from conversations they had in December of 2015.

O-games — The Olympic Games are international sporting events held every four years.

Oldfag — Slang term for a longtime 4chan, 8chan, or 8kun user.

OO — The Oval Office, which is the working office space of the President of the United States, located in the West Wing of the White House.

OP — Usually stands for "original poster," the person who originally published the thread on 4chan, 8chan, or 8kun. Occasionally it stands for "operation" as in a military or intelligence operation.

Operator — A person involved in an intelligence, military or other operation backed by a government or non-government entity.

OPS — Abbreviation for "Operations" such as military or intelligence operations.

Orig — Abbreviation for origin, original, originally.

OS — Congressional Oversight Committee

O-WH — The Obama White House

Owl — Occult symbol found throughout history.

over/under — An over-under or over/under bet is a wager in which a sportsbook will predict a number for a statistic in a given game, and bettors wager that the actual number in the game will be either higher or lower than that number.

P — Multiple uses: may refer to the Pope, but Q suggested it may also refer to the Payseurs—the descendants of the French Royal family who emigrated to the U.S. after the French Revolution. In more recent posts, it seems to indicate FBI agent Joe Pientka, who interviewed General Michael Flynn when he served as President Trump's National Security Advisor.

P_2020 — The 2020 Presidential election.

P_elec — Presidential election.

Pain or **[PAIN]** — A reference to the pending prosecution of corrupt individuals.

Painted — Some military weapon systems use lasers to guide missiles and bombs to their targets. When a target is illuminated by a laser, it is said to be "painted." As Q uses the term, it refers to corrupt people being identified for exposure or prosecution.

Paul Manafort — A businessman, lobbyist, and Member of Donald Trump's 2016 Presidential campaign. He was convicted of money laundering, tax evasion and failing to register as a foreign agent.

Paul Nakasone — The Lieutenant General who succeeded Admiral Michael Rogers as the Director of U.S. Cyber Command and NSA.

Pawn — An individual who is used by influential people to accomplish their objectives.

Pay-for-play — Bribery of a public official. Something of value is exchanged for an action taken by a public official. Sometimes expressed as "pay-to-play."

P_debates — Presidential debates

PEOC — Presidential Emergency Operations Center, an underground bunker-like structure beneath the East Wing of the White House.

Peter Strzok — FBI agent who was involved in the bureau's counterintelligence investigation of Presidential candidate Donald Trump. He was also a member of Special Counsel Robert Mueller's team until it was disclosed that he harbored an excessive bias against Trump. Strzok was one of the FBI agents who questioned Hillary Clinton regarding her emails, and he interviewed Lt. General Mike Flynn regarding his communications with Russian Ambassador Sergey Kislyak.

PG — Pizzagate/PedoGate, an internet controversy that surfaced in 2016, where restaurant owner James Alefantis and John Podesta were accused of pedophilia.

Glossary

Phase [2] — The second phase of a covert operation that Q mentioned on February 21st, 2018.

Pickle — A euphemism that describes a difficult or messy situation with no obvious solution.

Pickle Factory — A term used for the CIA.

Placeholder — A current post that alludes to details which will be disclosed in a future post.

Planefag — Slang term for a 4chan, 8chan, or 8kun user who specializes in tracking airplanes by radar.

PM — Prime Minister

Prev — An abbreviation for previous or prevent.

POTUS — President of the United States. As Q uses the term, it specifically refers to Donald J. Trump.

pp — People

PP — Planned Parenthood, the largest abortion provider in the United States, is a highly controversial organization with ardent supporters as well as staunch opponents.

P_PERS — A personal message from President Trump.

PR1 — Priority one, or top priority.

Prince Al-Waleed — Alwaleed bin Talal, a billionaire and philanthropist who was arrested November 4th, 2017, as part of the Saudi corruption crackdown.

PRISM — Surveillance program used by the NSA.

Priv — Abbreviation for private, privilege.

PRO — Meaning "in favor of." Examples: O-PRO is supportive of Barack Obama, PRO-POTUS is supportive of President Trump.

PROJECT DEEPDREAM — A reference to a Jason Bourne film in which a social media company called Deep Dream, gathers personal data from subscribers and secretly funnels it to the Central Intelligence Agency.

PSYOP — Psychological Operations, which convey selected information and indicators to audiences in order to influence their emotions, motives, objective reasoning, and ultimately their behavior.

Punisher skull — Marvel Comics' superhero Frank Castle (The Punisher) typically wears a shirt with a skull emblazoned on the chest. The skull logo was unofficially adopted by some military special operations teams and has been posted by Q.

Puppet — An individual controlled by global elites.

PVG — Pudong International Airport in Shanghai, China.

Q Clearance — Access to the highest level of classified information in the U.S. Department of Energy. Q suggested in his case, it refers to the highest level of access across all departments.

Q Clearance Patriot — The term "Q Clearance Patriot" first appeared on November 1st, 2017, where Q introduced himself with this name and the initial Q.

Quid Pro Quo — A Latin phrase indicating something given or received for something else. In cases of public bribery, something of value is exchanged for an action taken by a public official.

R — In most contexts, a reference to Renegade, the Secret Service code name for President Barack Obama. Other uses are possible.

R's — Republicans

Rachel Brand — U.S. Associate Attorney General from May 22nd, 2017, until February 20th, 2018. Resigned to take a job as head of global corporate governance at Walmart.

Glossary

Rapid Fire — A 1992 film starring Brandon Lee and Powers Booth, who battle a Chinese drug lord and corrupt FBI officials.

RBG — The late Ruth Bader Ginsburg was an Associate Justice of the U.S. Supreme Court. She was a liberal noted for her feminist views.

RC — Rachel "Ray" Chandler, photographer who co-founded Midland modeling Agency with Walter Pearce.

R+D — Republicans and Democrats

Rec — Usually stands for received, but occasionally stands for record.

RED1, RED2, RED3 — From a post on June 4th, 2020. These codes appear to indicate a predictable progression of events that may be taken by bad actors and the planned response by members of the military.

RED_CASTLE — Refers to the insignia of the U.S. Army Corps of Engineers.

Red Cross — The International or American Red Cross.

Red Line — A metaphor describing a condition which, if met, will trigger a response.

Red October — Multiple meanings: the film by that title; and a steel plant in Russia (which appears on a CIA document that Q referenced). Note: Q removed "the Hunt for," and in October of 2018, a new theme "Red October" appeared.

Red pill — A reference from the film *The Matrix*. Taking the red pill causes one to awaken to a different reality.

Red Red — The International or American Red Cross.

Re_drop — A re-post of an older message, usually for the benefit of people who are new followers.

Renee J. James — A tech executive, who was formerly the President of Intel. She is Chairman and CEO of Ampere Computing and an Operating Executive with The Carlyle Group in its Media and Technology practice.

Renegade — The Secret Service code name for President Barack Obama.

Repost Lost — When a post has been deleted from the board, Q will sometimes repost it with this notice.

Rig for Red — A term used by submariners when the vessel is coming to periscope depth. Red lights are illuminated providing enough light to see while maintaining night vision. In most cases, Q does not post for several days following a Rig for Red message.

Rizvi Traverse Management — The secretive New York private equity firm founded by Indian-born Suhail Rizvi. Investments include ICM Talent Agency, Summit Entertainment, Playboy Enterprises, SpaceX, Flipboard, and Square. Rizvi Traverse was the largest initial stakeholder of Twitter and was instrumental in bringing on board other investors like JP Morgan Chase and Alwaleed bin Talal. At Twitter's Initial Public Offering in 2013, Rizvi Traverse held a 15.6 percent stake in the company valued at $3.8 billion.

RM — Robert Mueller, Special Counsel who investigated President Donald Trump. Served as FBI Director from 2001-2013.

RNC — Republican National Committee, the governing body for the United States Republican Party.

Road block — Using the U.S. Military at the Mexico border to disrupt illegal entry, drugs, cash, terrorists, human trafficking, and MS-13 gang members.

ROASTED — A reference to President Trump's participation in the Gridiron Roast Dinner on March 4th, 2018.

Robert Byrd — Former U.S. Democrat Senator from West Virginia. Byrd was the longest-serving U.S. Senator in history. According to *Wikipedia*, in the early 1940s, he recruited 150 of his friends and associates to create a new chapter of the Ku Klux Klan in Sophia, West Virginia. Byrd partook in a lengthy filibuster effort against the 1964 Civil Rights Act. Hillary Clinton said Byrd was her mentor in the Senate. Joe Biden spoke at Byrd's funeral.

rogue1_McMaster — Former National Security Advisor H.R McMaster, who Q says was secretly sympathetic to the deep state.

Glossary

rogue2_Coats_DNI — Former Director of National Intelligence Dan Coats, who Q says was secretly sympathetic to the deep state.

Rogue3-6 — Unidentified deep state sympathizers who were installed early on that made referrals to President Trump to hire H.R. McMaster, Dan Coats, Christopher Wray, and John Bolton.

rogue7_Bolton — Former National Security Advisor John Bolton, who Q says was secretly sympathetic to the deep state.

Rosatom — A Russian state-owned energy company that purchased the North American company, Uranium One, during Barack Obama's presidency.

ROT — Rotation. A different view provided by the rotation of a camera.

ROTH — Rothschild

Rothschild — An influential banking family that exerted economic and political influence over Europe during the 18th and 19th centuries and over the world during the 20th and 21st centuries.

Rouhani — Hassan Rouhani, an Iranian politician who served as the seventh President of Iran from 2013 to 2021.

RR — Former U.S. Deputy Attorney General Rod Rosenstein. He conducted oversight of Robert Mueller's investigation of President Donald Trump.

RT — Multiple possible meanings including retweet, real-time, the news outlet *Russia Today*, and former Secretary of State Rex Tillerson. The context will dictate the best decode.

Running RED — A phrase first used on September 19, 2020 in reference to the upcoming battle to confirm President Trump's selection for the Supreme Court, Amy Coney Barrett. The suggestion was that Barrett would be confirmed, despite the battle that would be waged. The phrase was used again the following day as the last line of a post, suggesting that it could be considered a Q signature.

Ryan — Paul Ryan, former Wisconsin Representative and former Speaker of the U.S. House of Representatives.

SA — The Kingdom of Saudi Arabia

SA --> US --> Asia --> EU — A flow chart showing an order of operations. According to Q, the removal of corruption began in Saudi Arabia and will then happen in the United States, followed by Asia, then the European Union, and other nations.

Sage — By entering the word "sage" in the email field on a 4chan, 8chan, or 8kun thread, you can comment on a thread without bumping it to the top of the board. (Typically used to comment on bad threads to avoid giving them more visibility.)

Sally Yates — Served as Deputy Attorney General under Barack Obama, and briefly as Attorney General under Donald Trump but was fired for insubordination.

Sam Clovis — A policy advisor to the Trump campaign in 2016.

SAP — Special Access Program, a security protocol used by the U.S. federal government that provides highly classified information with safeguards and access restrictions that exceed those used for regular classified information.

Sara — Sara A. Carter, a national and international award-winning investigative reporter who is currently a Fox News contributor.

Sauce — Slang term derived from the word "source." When information is provided on 4chan, 8chan, or 8kun that is not common knowledge, the one posting the information will frequently be asked to provide a source (sauce).

SB — Super Bowl, the annual championship game of the National Football League.

SC — Two confirmed decodes: Special Counsel, or the Supreme Court. The context will dictate the correct one.

SCARAMUCCI MODEL — Anthony Scaramucci served as President Trump's White House Director of Communications from July 21st to July 31st, 2017. During those ten days, Sean Spicer and Reince Priebus resigned. The point Q wants us to understand is that a temporary hire can accomplish unpleasant tasks easier that someone in a permanent position.

Glossary

Schneiderman — Eric Schneiderman, former New York state Attorney General who resigned May 7th, 2018, due to allegations of past sexual assault by four women.

SCI — Sensitive Compartmented Information. A protocol for securing highly sensitive information using control systems approved by the Director of National Intelligence.

SCI(f) or SCIF — Sensitive Compartmentalized Information Facility. An enclosed area that is used to process sensitive and classified information and restrict access to people who do not have the proper security clearance and need to know.

Scot-Free — A phrase used in a post by Q to indicate someone who goes unpunished, while also alluding to the motion picture studio Scott Free Productions that produced the film *White Squall*.

SD — State Department (formally called the U.S. Department of State). The department of the U.S. executive branch responsible for carrying out foreign policy and international relations.

SDNY — Southern District of New York, a powerful U.S. Attorney's office that controls the fate of many of the nation's important legal cases.

SEALS — Special forces teams of the U.S. Navy tasked with conducting small-unit special operation missions. The acronym comes from "Sea, Air, and Land."

SEC — In most cases, it refers to "secure" or "security," i.e., NAT SEC (National Security). In some cases, it refers to the Securities and Exchange Commission. The context will provide the correct decode.

SecureDrop — A program that allows intelligence community employees to communicate with journalists securely.

Sergey Brin — Sergey Mikhaylovich Brin, the Russian-born former President of Alphabet (the parent company of Google and YouTube). Brin co-founded the search engine firm Google with Larry Page in 1998.

Sessions — Jeff Sessions, former U.S. Senator from Alabama. Served as Attorney General under President Trump from 2017-2019.

SFO — San Francisco International Airport

SH — Steve Huffman is the founder and CEO of Reddit, an online discussion site. He is also known by his Reddit nickname "Spez."

SHADOW ARM — The term "arm" is used by Q in various ways to allude to the idea that the corporate media covertly act as the propaganda wing of the Democratic Party.

Shall we play a game? — A line spoken by a computer (WOPR, or War Operation Plan Response) to Matthew Broderick's character David in the 1983 film *War Games*. David thought he'd hacked a software developer and gained access to new games, but he unwittingly hacked into a Department of Defense system and nearly started a global thermonuclear war. Q uses the phrase in some cases to challenge anons and, in other instances, to taunt his enemies.

Shell1/Shell2 — A reference to "shell" companies. A shell company is a business created to hold the funds and manage the financial transactions of another entity. They don't have employees, don't make money, and don't provide customers with products or services. They only manage the assets they hold.

Shill — Someone who spends time and resources promoting (or attacking) a product or idea in public forums with the pretense of sincerity.

Shooter — A reference to the perpetrator of a mass shooting.

SID — Likely a reference to Arizona Senator John Sidney McCain III. A second possibility is Sid Blumenthal, a longtime confidant to Hillary Clinton.

Sidley Austin — Chicago-based law firm Sidley Austin LLP is the sixth-largest U.S.-based corporate law firm with approximately 2,000 lawyers and annual revenues of more than two billion dollars.

SIG — Multiple interpretations. Sometimes used as an abbreviation for signal. Also used as an abbreviation for Special Interest Group, a group of individuals, brought together by a shared interest, often aiming to influence politics or policies.

SIGINT — Signals Intelligence. The interception and decoding of electronic signals, whether used in communication between people or other applications (i.e., radar and weapon systems). Analysts evaluate raw electronic data and transform it into actionable intelligence.

Silent War — A phrase used once by Q in November of 2017, to indicate an ongoing, covert war against the principles of freedom and democracy in the U.S. In 2020, the phrase was used more regularly and became a Q signature that will be explored in depth in a future volume in this series.

SIS — Secret Intelligence Service, another name for the UK's MI6. This agency is the UK counterpart to the CIA. SIS was also the acronym used for the Signal Intelligence Service, the United States Army's codebreaking division, before World War II. It was renamed the Signal Security Agency in 1943, and in 1945, it became the Army Security Agency. During World War II, its resources were reassigned to the newly established National Security Agency (NSA).

SIT ROOM — Situation Room. Officially known as the John F. Kennedy Conference Room, the "Situation Room" is a conference room and intelligence management center in the basement of the White House run by the National Security Council staff for the use of the President and his advisors to monitor and deal with crises at home and abroad and to conduct secure communications with outside persons.

SKY EVENT or **SKY Event** — Q posted a reference to this twice, but has not confirmed a decode yet.

Sleeper — a term for someone who joins a community pretending to share their values, while secretly opposing them. At a strategic time—when the "sleeper" is signaled to "awaken" or become active—they carry out their covert mission of disruption or sabotage.

Smollett — Jussie Smollett, an American actor and singer, who was indicted on February 20th, 2019, for allegedly paying two Nigerian-Americans to stage a fake hate crime assault on him.

Sniffer or **Sniffers** — Generally, a bot designed to search the internet for specific data on websites. Q has alluded to highly sophisticated artificial intelligence programs that aggregate data and interpret it. Valerie Jarret has also been identified by Q as a "sniffer."

Snopes — A fact-checking organization that produces reports on rumors, urban legends, and odd news stories. Snopes has been criticized for its liberal-progressive bias.

Snowden — Edward Snowden, the former CIA employee and NSA contractor who stole and made public two classified NSA surveillance programs—PRISM and XKeyscore.

Snow White — A signature by Q referring to the CIA, so named because of the Agency's seven supercomputers that are named after the seven dwarves.

SOCIALM — Social media.

Soros — George Soros, a hedge fund billionaire who is known for using his wealth to fund his own brand of political activism. Recipients of his philanthropy appreciate his money, but those who oppose his political views see him as a creator of chaos around the world—a destabilizing force on economies and societies. Some countries have either banned Soros or restricted his organizations. These countries include Pakistan, Poland, Turkey, Russia, Soros' home country of Hungary, and the Philippines. The Israeli government has said Soros is not welcome there.

SOTU — The annual State of the Union speech given by the President of the United States.

SP — Samantha Power, U.S. Ambassador to the United Nations from 2013 to 2017.

Spade — Katherine Noel Brosnahan, known professionally as Kate Spade and Kate Valentine. She was a fashion designer and businesswoman, who founded the designer brand "Kate Spade New York." Spade's death in June of 2017 was ruled a suicide. She was reported to have hung herself from a doorknob using a red silk scarf.

Spartans in Darkness — "Spartans in Darkness: American SIGINT and the Indochina War, 1945-1975" is a report written by Robert J. Hanyok, of the Center for Cryptologic History, National Security Agency. A link to the document was posted by Q as reference material.

Glossary

Speed — A film starring Keanu Reeves and Sandra Bullock about a bus that had a bomb connected to the speedometer by a villain. If the bus speed dropped below 50 miles per hour, the bomb would detonate. The conundrum for the hero was how to defuse the bomb without stopping the bus. "Speed" is used as a signature by Q to indicate a delicate situation involving corrupt people that is being dealt with by patriots in a way that will avoid unnecessary harm to the public and keep government services open.

Spirit Cooking — (from *Wikipedia*) Marina Abramovic worked with Jacob Samuel to produce a cookbook of "aphrodisiac recipes" called Spirit Cooking in 1996. These "recipes" were meant to be "evocative instructions for actions or for thoughts." For example, one of the recipes calls for "13,000 grams of jealousy," while another says to "mix fresh breast milk with fresh sperm milk." The work was inspired by the popular belief that ghosts feed off intangible things like light, sound, and emotions.

In 1997, Abramovic created a multimedia Spirit Cooking installation. This was originally installed in the Zerynthia Associazione per l'Arte Contemporanea in Rome, Italy and included white gallery walls with "enigmatically violent recipe instructions" painted in pig's blood. According to Alexxa Gotthardt, the work is "a comment on humanity's reliance on ritual to organize and legitimize our lives and contain our bodies."

Abramovic also published a Spirit Cooking cookbook, containing comico-mystical, self-help instructions that are meant to be just poetry. Spirit Cooking later evolved into a form of dinner party entertainment that Abramovic occasionally lays on for collectors, donors, and friends.

Spider web — A metaphor that describes a web of deceit. Literal spider webs were painted on a building in Syria that was visited by Senator John McCain.

Splash — A Naval aviator term for shooting down an enemy aircraft. An airplane shot down over the ocean will "splash" into the sea.

Spygate — The scandal that grew out of the FBI surveillance by the Obama administration of Donald Trump's 2016 Presidential campaign. After investigating what the media widely called a "conspiracy theory," U.S. Attorney John Durham wrote a comprehensive report that confirmed much of what anons already understood from their own research.

spy_T — The government spying operation against President Donald Trump.

SR — There are two confirmed decodes, both of which would depend on the context of the post: Barack Obama's National Security Advisor Susan Rice, and Seth Rich, the Democratic National Committee staffer who was murdered in Washington D.C. on July 10th, 2016.

SS — U.S. Secret Service, a federal law enforcement agency under the Department of Homeland Security charged with conducting criminal investigations and protecting the nation's leaders and their families.

Standard Hotel — The Standard Hotels are a group of five boutique hotels in Los Angeles (Hollywood and Downtown LA), New York City, and Miami Beach. Q's references pertain to the Hollywood location.

Stanislav Lunev — A former Soviet military officer who defected to the United States in 1992. He is the highest-ranking GRU (Russian intelligence) officer ever to defect to the United States. He has worked with the CIA and FBI and is currently in the federal witness protection program.

Stormy Daniels — A pornographic actress, stripper, screenwriter, and director. In 2018, Daniels became involved in a legal dispute with President Trump and his attorney Michael Cohen. Daniels claimed that Trump and his surrogates paid $130,000 in hush money to silence her about an affair she says she had with Trump in 2006. Trump's spokespeople have denied the affair and have accused Daniels of lying.

Strike Package — As used by the military, a strike package is a group of aircraft having different weaponry and capabilities that are launched as a unit to perform a single attack mission.

Sum of All Fears — A Q signature and a reference to the Tom Clancy novel and film by that name. The plot: a sociopath develops a plan to get Russia and the U.S. to destroy each other in a nuclear war, paving the way for him to set up a fascist superstate.

super T — Super Tuesday. The first Tuesday in March, when a large number of states hold their Presidential primary elections.

Glossary

SURV — Surveillance

Susan Rice — U.S. National Security Advisor for Barack Obama from 2013 to 2017, who also as U.S. Ambassador to the United Nations from 2009 to 2013.

Swamp — Washington D.C., which is rumored to have been built on a swamp. Research more at Histories of the National Mall: http://mallhistory.org/explorations/show/was-the-national-mall-built-on

T2 — Terminal 2 at Shanghai Pudong International Airport (PVG).

Taken — A 2008 film about a retired CIA agent who traveled across Europe relying on his knowledge of tradecraft to save his estranged daughter, who, along with her girlfriend, was kidnapped by Albanian sex traffickers.

target C — This appears to be Q's way of indicating that Ted Cruz's Presidential campaign was targeted for surveillance by the Obama administration.

target POTUS — Q's way of indicating that Donald Trump's Presidential campaign was targeted for surveillance by the Obama administration.

TG — Trey Gowdy, former South Carolina Representative and former federal prosecutor who served as Chair of the House Oversight and Government Reform Committee.

The Analysis Corporation (TAC) — A corporation founded in 1991 in McClean, Virginia, by Cecilia Hayes. TAC works on projects in the counterterrorism and national security industries. John Brennan was appointed TAC President and CEO in 2005.

The Bloody Wonderland — Q's reference to Saudi Arabia, which was notorious in the past for its frequent use of public execution.

The Farm — Central Intelligence Agency training facility.

TheMagikBOT — A *Wikipedia* bot that makes automated or semi-automated edits to *Wikipedia* entries that would be difficult to do manually.

T logs —Transaction logs.

TOR — An internet browsing service that allows users to view web pages anonymously by routing traffic through an overlay network made up of thousands of relays.

TP — Tony Podesta, an influential Washington D.C. lobbyist who stepped down from his firm, The Podesta Group, as a result of Special Counsel Mueller's investigation and the firm's unregistered lobbying for the European Centre for Modern Ukraine. Podesta Group failed to file as an agent of a foreign power under the Foreign Agents Registration Act (FARA). Tony is the brother of John Podesta, the chairman of the 2016 Hillary Clinton Presidential campaign.

TRI — Triangle, usually indicates the three wealthiest families; the House of Saud, the Rothschilds and George Soros.

Trip, Tripcode or **Trip code** — A hashed password used on internet boards like 4chan, 8chan, or 8kun that provides a unique user identity while maintaining anonymity.

Trump Swift Boat Project — An operation by Hillary Clinton's campaign in 2016 designed to smear her political opponent Donald Trump. It was mentioned in an email exchange published by *WikiLeaks*.

TSA — Transportation Security Administration, an agency of the United States Department of Homeland Security created as a response to the September 11th attacks. The TSA has authority over the security of the traveling public in the United States.

TT — Two confirmed decodes. The context will determine the correct one. It can refer to Trump Tower in New York. It can also be an abbreviation for Tarmac Tapes. According to Q, the NSA has a recording (tape) of the conversation that Bill Clinton had with then-Attorney General Loretta Lynch on the tarmac at Sky Harbor Airport in Phoenix, Arizona, on June 27th, 2016.

TTM — Trailing twelve months, or the twelve months that follow.

T-Tower — Trump Tower. A skyscraper on Fifth Avenue, between 56th and 57th Streets, in Midtown Manhattan, New York City. Trump Tower serves as the headquarters for the Trump Organization.

Glossary

U1 — An abbreviation for the North American company, Uranium One, which was sold to the Russian energy company, Rosatom.

U1 -> CA -> EU -> ASIA -> IRAN/NK — According to Q, this is the route of travel for uranium transferred when the company, Uranium One, was sold to the Russian company, Rosatom: from Canada, to the European Union, to Asia, to Iran/North Korea.

UBL — Usama bin Laden (AKA Osama bin Laden) was a founder of the pan-Islamic militant organization al-Qaeda.

Uhuru Kenyatta — Kenyan politician and the fourth President of the Republic of Kenya.

UID — User ID for internet connection or specific internet-connected device.

UK/AUS assist/set up — According to Q, the UK and Australia, through the Five Eyes agreement, assisted the Obama administration in surveilling Donald Trump's Presidential campaign.

Unmask — To expose the concealed name of a U.S. person incidentally caught up in routine surveillance of foreign officials.

UN — United Nations, an intergovernmental organization responsible for facilitating cooperation in international law, international security, economic development, diplomacy and human rights. It was founded in 1945 to replace the League of Nations.

Upstream collection — A term used by the National Security Agency for intercepting email, telephone, and text message data from the major internet cables and switches, both domestic and foreign.

US — The United States of America

US ATT — U.S. Attorney

USA V. [1-2-3-6] — A reference to future legal cases where currently unidentified people will be named as defendants in cases against the United States.

US Cyber Task Force — In February of 2018, Attorney General Jeff Sessions ordered the creation of the Justice Department's Cyber-Digital Task Force, which "will canvass the many ways that the Department is combatting the global cyber threat, and will also identify how federal law enforcement can more effectively accomplish its mission in this vital and evolving area."

USD(I) — The Under Secretary of Defense for Intelligence

US-G — United States Government

USMC — United States Marine Corps, a branch of the U.S. Armed Forces responsible for conducting expeditionary and amphibious operations with the Navy, the Army, and the Air Force.

USMIL / US M's – United States military.

USSS — United States Secret Service, a federal law enforcement agency under the Department of Homeland Security charged with conducting criminal investigations and protecting the nation's leaders and their families.

v2 — Version 2: a reference to the second term of Donald Trump's presidency. The implication is that it will be run differently than his first term.

Vault 7 — A series of documents published by *WikiLeaks* in 2017 that detail the capabilities of the CIA to perform electronic surveillance and cyber warfare. The files, dated from 2013–2016, include details on the agency's software capabilities, such as the ability to compromise cars, smart TVs, web browsers, and the operating systems of most smartphones, as well as operating systems like Microsoft Windows, MacOS, and Linux.

Vindman — Retired Lieutenant Colonel Alexander Vindman, a member of the National Security Council who testified against President Trump during the House impeachment hearings.

VIP — Very Important Person. Usually a reference to people who wear Q related shirts at President Trump's rallies. On a few occasions, the President has pointed to these patriots in the crowd. Many VIPs have posted rally photos on Twitter. Q has reposted links to them on the board.

Glossary

VJ — Valerie Jarrett, a businesswoman and former government official who served as the senior advisor to U.S. President Barack Obama. Jarrett was born in Iran to African-American parents; her family moved to London for a year, and then to Chicago in 1963.

VP — Vice President.

W&W — Wizards and warlocks; an internal name used by NSA employees and contractors—guardians of all electronic information.

WASH — An abbreviation for Washington D.C.

We don't say his name — John McCain, U.S. Senator from Arizona. He served as a Senator from January 1987 until his death in 2018.

Wendy — Nickname for Maggie Nixon. The daughter of Sarah Nixon and granddaughter of actress and TV soap opera writer and producer Agnes Nixon.

Wet Works — Slang for assassination. The term was used in the John Podesta emails published by *WikiLeaks*.

Wexner — Les Wexner, the billionaire founder and former CEO of Victoria's Secret parent company L Brands. Wexner was a confidant of Jeffrey Epstein.

WH — White House, the official residence and workplace of the President of the United States. White House is also used as a metonym for the President and his advisors.

Wheels up — An aviation term indicating an aircraft is taking off, and its landing gear are being retracted. Q used this term as a signal that an individual he referred to as the "stealth bomber" was commencing operations.

Where we go one, we go all — A line from the film *White Squall* which was based on the sinking of a school Brigantine sailing ship in 1961. The phrase "Where we go one, we go all" is a signature found in many of Q's posts.

Whistleblower — Q is usually referring to the whistleblower who filed a complaint to the Intelligence Community Inspector General about President Trump's phone call to the President of Ukraine.

White Squall — A 1996 coming of age film in which a group of high school and college-aged misfits sign up for training aboard a sailing ship under the instruction of a hard but courageous skipper. Scenes from the film have been highlighted by Q as themes that illustrate different aspects of his mission.

WHO — World Health Organization

Who performs in a circus? — Clowns, which is a reference to the CIA, an agency Q also refers to as "Clowns In America."

WikiLeaks — A watchdog organization founded by Julian Assange that publishes documents leaked from various government and corporate sources.

Wizards & Warlocks — An internal name used by NSA employees and contractors—guardians of all electronic information.

WL — *WikiLeaks,* a watchdog organization founded by Julian Assange that publishes documents leaked from various government and corporate sources.

Woodshed — Nickname for the White House Situation Room, a 5,000 square foot complex of rooms in the ground floor of the West Wing.

Wray — Christopher Wray, Director of the FBI.

WRWY — We are with you.

WW — World Wide

WWG1WGA — The abbreviation for "Where we go one, we go all," a line from the film *White Squall* which was based on the sinking of a school Brigantine sailing ship in 1961. The phrase "Where we go one, we go all" is a signature found in many of Q's posts.

Y — Generally, refers to the goat head and owl symbolism, images, and icons used by the occult. It has also been used in references to former FBI Director James Come[Y] and with reference to his book, A Higher Loyalty [Y]. Sometimes, it signifies "yes."

Glossary

YT — YouTube, an American video-sharing platform headquartered in California that now operates as one of Google's subsidiaries.

Zero Bubble — Used in submarine operations when a vessel's stern (rear) and bow (front) are at the same depth, with no incline. In Q's vernacular, it goes along with Rig for Red, coming to periscope depth. Both seem to be related to his frequency of posting.

Zero Delta — A term used to signify posts by Q and President Trump that occur at the same time.

Other Books from Dave Hayes / Praying Medic
Find all current titles on PrayingMedic.com

Series: Q Chronicles
- Book 1 - The Calm Before The Storm
- Book 2 - The Great Awakening
- Book 3 - This Is Not a Game

Series: The Kingdom of God Made Simple
- Divine Healing Made Simple
- Seeing in the Spirit Made Simple
- Hearing God's Voice Made Simple
- Traveling in the Spirit Made Simple
- Dream Interpretation Made Simple

Series: The Courts of Heaven

- Defeating Your Adversary in the Court of Heaven
- Operating in the Court of Angels

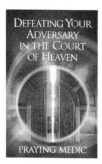 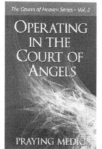

Series: My Craziest Adventures with God

- My Craziest Adventures with God - Volume 1
- My Craziest Adventures with God - Volume 2

And more...

- Emotional Healing in 3 Easy Steps
- The Gates of Shiloh (novel)
- God Speaks: Perspectives on Hearing God's Voice
- A Kingdom View of Economic Collapse
- American Sniper: Lessons in Spiritual Warfare

Made in the USA
Las Vegas, NV
11 February 2024